Major J. W. Ratchford
Circa March 1872

SOME REMINISCENCES OF PERSONS AND INCIDENTS OF THE CIVIL WAR

by
James Wylie Ratchford
Assistant Adjutant-General in the Confederate Army

To Which is Appended
THE CONFEDERATE SOLDIER IN THE RANKS
An Address by
Major-General D. H. Hill, C. S. A.

THE CONFEDERATE REPRINT COMPANY

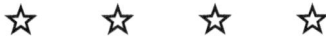

☆   ☆   ☆   ☆

WWW.CONFEDERATEREPRINT.COM

Some Reminiscences of Persons
and Incidents of the Civil War
by James Wylie Ratchford

Originally Published in 1909
by Whittet and Shepperson, Printers
Richmond, Virginia

Reprint Edition © 2015
The Confederate Reprint Company
Post Office Box 2027
Toccoa, Georgia 30577
www.confederatereprint.com

Cover and Interior by
Magnolia Graphic Design
www.magnoliagraphicdesign.com

ISBN-13: 978-0692452233
ISBN-10: 0692452230

CONTENTS

☆   ☆   ☆   ☆

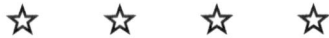

CHAPTER ONE
Bethel Regiment

☆　　☆　　☆　　☆

I shall begin these reminiscences with the statement (certainly true so far as I have been able to learn), that mine was the first blood shed in an open engagement in the late Civil War.

My connection with the Confederate Army began as lieutenant and drill master in the First Regiment North Carolina Volunteers, now historically known as "The Bethel Regiment," on account of the signal service it rendered in the Bethel fight, the first pitched battle of the war.

This regiment was composed of the flower of the North Carolina troops, and for the service during its short career as a regiment, and the number and efficiency of the officers it furnished other regiments after its disbandment, it has no peer on the roll of gallant Southern regiments.

The Organization of the Regiment

I was a cadet in the North Carolina Military Institute when in April, 1861, Governor Ellis, of North Carolina, invited D.H. Hill, then superintendent of the Military

Institute, to take charge of the Camp of Instruction, and drill the troops which were gathering at Raleigh. He accepted the invitation, and set out immediately for Raleigh, taking with him all his faculty and about one hundred cadets.

Troops from all over the State were pouring in and after several weeks of drilling the first regiment was organized. There were more than one hundred companies of fine men in camp, and all were anxious to be included in the first regiment sent out, for the opinion prevailed that the war would be a matter of only a few weeks, and were anxious to see some of the fighting before it should be over.

The Personnel of the Regiment

The honor fell upon ten companies of picked troops. Historic Charlotte was represented by two companies, the Hornet's Nest Rifles, an organization which had come down from Revolutionary times, under Captain Owens, and the Charlotte Grays, a company made up and officered by boys under or near twenty-one years of age, under Captain Ross. There was a company from Buncombe county under Captain McDowell, one from Burke county, under Captain Avery – all fit men, averaging one hundred and sixty-five pounds each – one company from Tarborough, commanded by Captain Bridges, one from Orange, under Captain Ashe, two companies from Fayetteville, under Captains Hunt and —, and one from Lincoln, under Captain Hoke. These, officers and privates, were above the average in intelligence, ability, and worth of character as is shown by their records throughout the war.

The Charlotte companies, coming as they did, from

the "Hornet's Nest" of Revolutionary heroes, inherited the spirit as well as the blood of those same heroes. The greater part of these were of old Presbyterian families whose faith had come pure from the highlands of Scotland, and they were men whose religion was so inseparable from the details of their lives as to enable them to remain calm and deliberate in the midst of flying bullets and shells whose course was directed by an all-wise God.

But the glory of the regiment was Colonel D.H. Hill (afterwards lieutenant-general). A scholarly gentleman and gallant soldier, he possessed in a high degree the qualities of leadership which inspired the utmost confidence and loyalty in his soldiers and made him the idol of the Carolinas.

He graduated from West Point in the class with Longstreet, Rosecrans, and other distinguished officers in both armies. Upon his graduation, he was assigned to the artillery of the United States Army, and served with such distinction in the Mexican War, that he was twice brevetted on the field of battle for gallant and meritorious conduct, and the Legislature of South Carolina voted him a sword.

Some fifteen years before the outbreak of sectional hostilities, he resigned his commission in the United States Army, and engaged in educational work. For six years he filled with distinguished ability the chair of Mathematics in Washington College (now Washington and Lee University), Virginia. It was through his influence that Stonewall Jackson was elected to the faculty of the Virginia Military Institute. For six years more he filled the chair of Mathematics in Davidson College, North Carolina, and then two years superintendent of the North Carolina Military Institute at Charlotte.

He was the author of several scholarly books, one of them being a work on Algebra, which for years was used as a text-book in institutions throughout the South.

He was a brother-in-law of Stonewall Jackson, who repeatedly declared in my hearing that there was not in a man in the Southern Army superior in military genius to D.H. Hill, and emphatically expressed his disgust at the politics and bickerings that prevented the repeated gallantry of Hill and the brilliant services rendered by him from being officially recognized and rewarded. I remember General Hill's reply to such a speech on one occasion, and I give it as truly typical of his pure patriotism and unselfish willingness to sacrifice his own glory to the service of his country. With a tinge of reproach in his manner he said, "I am not fighting Mr. Davis' battles, and if I am not permitted to serve my country as a general officer, I will as a private."

There can be made no better commentary on the greatness of the two men than their mutual admiration and love. Hill respected and loved Jackson for the nobility and beauty of character which he recognized under a rather uncouth exterior, while Jackson's admiration of Hill and his gratitude for his many services was unbounded.

Though the taciturnity and uncommunicativeness of Jackson in regard to his military plans has passed into a proverb, whenever the opportunity offered itself he sought counsel of Hill as of his own mind.

In their deeply religious natures, these two men had a kinship closer than that of marriage. Jackson's faith and habits of prayer were not more widely known and respected among the troops than those of Hill. Though he was unobtrusive in his views, his faith was so much a part of himself as to be felt by those about him, just as much as his keen humor, which was the delight of the army circles and which often came out even in his official reports. Few are the narratives written by his brother officers, which are without one or more of the half-affectionate jokes of his piety, which was current among the soldiers.

Our lieutenant-colonel was the gallant C. C. Lee, who as colonel of another regiment, was killed in the fight at Hanover Court House. He was the son of the old North Carolina Colonel S. D Lee, another illustrious kinsman of the Virginia Lees. He had been the first honor man of his class at West Point, but had left the army, and at the time of his election was professor in the North Carolina Military Institute.

Our major too, was one of the old institute professors, James H. Lane, first honor man from the Virginia Military Institute, and later brigadier-general. Though he was still under thirty years of age, he was exceedingly bald. Once, on being chaffed on this score he made a reply which passed into a classic among the cadets. It was to the effect that he dwelt on a higher plane than his more hirsute friends, there being not a hair between him and heaven.

Moved to Seat of War

About the first of May, 1861, we were ordered by Governor Ellis to the seat of war, and left the Camp of Instruction, the envy of the companies left behind. At Richmond we were received with great demonstrations of honor and welcome, being visited in camp by crowds of ladies bringing flowers and delicacies.

We went from Richmond to West Point by rail and from there to Yorktown by boat. It was on this voyage that Lieutenant Poteat's horse indulged a most peculiar whim. Falling overboard as we were crossing the neck of the sea, he swam steadily outward until he seemed to be only the merest speck, and then turned around and swam directly back to the boat where he was picked up.

I Make the Acquaintance of Colonel Magruder

Upon our arrival at Yorktown, we reported to Colonel Magruder who was in charge of the Department of the Peninsula.

I was sent by Colonel Hill to report our arrival to Colonel Magruder, and set out on my errand with fear and trembling, for I had all of a boy's awe for those in high places. It was not at all reassuring to be halted by a sentinel when I reached the gate of the house where the commander was making his headquarters. I got past him only to fall into the clutches of an orderly at the door, for Colonel Magruder having a natural bent towards pomposity, rigidly kept up all the ceremony to which he had been accustomed in the old army. I had no time to compose my nerves after this interview before I found myself in the presence of the commander himself. Nor was his dignified and rather pompous military bearing such as to inspire confidence and self-possession in a lieutenant not yet accustomed to his own rank.

I remember distinctly, his smoking jacket with its great lapels turning back, and showing the rich crimson lining. I had never considered a smoking jacket an awe-inspiring sight, but that gorgeous garment gave me much the same impression as if it had been a robe of state. Yet his manner was courteously kind, and by the time my message was delivered, I was so far at ease with him as to accept with pleasure the invitation to have a julep with him.

Life in Camp

Though there were several companies of cavalry scattered over the peninsula, we were the first troops at Yorktown, and immediately set to work, drilling our soldiers, and fortifying the place. Soon other troops came in; there were Drew's Battalion and Coppen's Battalion of Zouaves, both from New Orleans, a regiment from Louisiana and another North Carolina regiment. This is a low, flat country; the weather was hot and the water was bad, yet the men kept in good spirits, and there was no grumbling at the hard drill and harder work.

Skirmishes Around Bethel

The Federals, twelve thousand strong, were stationed at Fortress Monroe and Hampton, under the command of General B. F. Butler. From these headquarters marauding parties continually overran the country, robbing, burning and killing.

Colonel Magruder ordered Colonel Hill to take his regiment and punish the marauders. On the 6th of June, Colonel Hill with the First North Carolina Regiment of Volunteers, and four pieces of Randolph's Battalion of the Richmond Howitzers, left Yorktown, and on the next day reached Bethel Church, twelve miles from Hampton.

This place we proceeded to fortify, and make the headquarters for putting a stop to the depredation of the marauders. In his official report, Colonel Hill gives a graphic account of the incidents of the next two days:

> We had only twenty-five spades, six axes, and three picks, but these were busily plied all day and night of the 7th and all day on the 8th. On the afternoon of the 8th, I learned that a marauding party of the enemy was

within a few miles of us.

I called for a party of thirty-four men to drive them back. Lieutenant Roberts, of Company F, of my regiment, promptly responded, and in five minutes his command was enroute. I detached Major Randolph with one howitzer to join them, and Lieutenant-Colonel Lee, First Regiment North Carolina Volunteers, requested and was granted permission to take command of the whole. After a march of five miles they came across the marauders busy over the spoils of a plundered house. A shell soon put the plunderers to flight, and they were chased over the New Market Bridge, where our little force was halted, in consequence of the presence of a considerable body situated on the other side. Lieutenant-Colonel Lee brought in one prisoner. How many of the enemy were killed and wounded is not known. None of our command was hurt. Soon after Lieutenant-Colonel Lee left, a citizen came dashing in with the information that seventy-five marauders were on the Back River road. I called for Captain McDowell's company (E), of the First Regiment of North Carolina Volunteers, and in three minutes it was in hot pursuit. Lieutenant West, of the Howitzer Battalion, with one piece, was detached to join them, and Major Lane, of my regiment, volunteered to assume the command of the whole. After a weary march they encountered, dispersed, and chased the wretches over the New Market Bridge, this being the second race on the same day over the New Market course, in both of which the Yankees reached the goal first. Major Lane brought in one prisoner. Reliable citizens reported that two cart loads and one buggy load of wounded were taken into Hampton. We had not a single man killed or wounded.

The Fight

On the 9th, Colonel Magruder came up and assumed command. Colonel Hill was ordered to set out early the following morning and march towards Fortress Monroe, by way of a dare (as it seemed to me) to the enemy.

A battle now seemed imminent, and the prospect had now none of its hazy fascination of a month before. All my previous experience of the use of firearms had been in hunting small game, when a large proportion of the shot took effect, and I felt sure my hours on earth were numbered. However, that night I heard a conversation between Colonels Hill and Magruder which was very comforting. They agreed that for one-fourth of the men engaged in a fight to be hit was a very heavy loss, and for one-fourth of those hit to be killed was a heavy mortality.

The rapidity of my mental calculation on my chances of life would have been the delight of Professor Hill in class-room days.

In obedience to orders, Colonel Hill set out towards Fortress Monroe at 3 o'clock on the morning of Monday the 10th. A heavy fog hung over the earth, so that even after we had marched some four miles, all objects were still enveloped in obscurity. At this stage of the march we met a lone woman walking. On being assured by our colonel that we were friends, she told him that only a short time before there had been a terrible battle in her yard.

At this time we were somewhat puzzled as to whom the combatants had been. We learned later that General Butler had ordered a party from Fortress Monroe, under General Pierce, and another from Hampton, under General Phelps to march before day, unite at the junction of the roads, and march on to Bethel, where they were to attack the Confederates, who were known to be there. These two parties, coming together in the dark, mistook each other for the enemy, and had quite a lively fight.

This warned us that we were within a few hundred yards of the enemy and we lost no time in falling back to our fortifications.

My Remembrance of the Battle

The enemy attacked our position about 9 o'clock, and as the firing began, all the assurance I had drawn from the conversation of the colonels the night before vanished as thin air, and when one of the first shells fired from the Federal batteries burst a few yards from me, literally tearing a mule to pieces, the one chance of being killed seemed much more imminent than the fifteen of escape.

When the enemy had driven our skirmishers in, and were feeling for the weak places in our line, Colonel Hill sent me several hundred yards to the left of our line to call in a company of pickets, who were in danger of being cut off from the main body of the army.

When I had left him, he and his field officers were mounted, and when I returned they were nowhere to be found. I now began to have a wild longing for the solitude of the woods, and I remember thinking that if only it were dark, I should lose no time in satisfying that longing; but stronger even than my fears was my knowledge of the fate that awaited cowards and shirkers at the hands of those at home, and feeling half-thankful, half-regretful for my regard for public opinion, I went about my duty with a great show of calmness.

I had not yet learned that when my superior officer dismounted, I was at liberty to do so too. I was the only man on horseback in sight, and the enemy, probably thinking me an officer of high rank, turned loose on me with grape and canister, until the sound or the missiles coming through the air, was like a covey of flying quail, rising from the ground. A shot grazed my temple. I felt very much as if it had taken half my head with it and I remembered raising my hand to feel how much was gone, and thinking how horrible I should look as a corpse. Then consciousness left me and I fell from my horse. The animal, fully sharing my longing for solitude, and not having my restraints, took to the woods. The last of the fight which I saw was the charge of the Federals, led by the gallant Major Winthrop, who was killed shortly after I was hit.

When I recovered consciousness, I was lying in the breastworks, a few yards from the spot where Major Winthrop had fallen. The enemy were gone, and there was no sound to be heard save the voice of the Negro cook, offering me coffee.

The Regiment's Part in the Battle

Being hit so early in the fight, I know but little of the action of the troops from personal observation. But the hero-worship accorded us while the details and impressions were fresh in the minds of the people are enough to assure me that our regiment's part in the battle was a glorious one, even without the words of warm praise and gratitude which found their way into even the official reports.

Colonel Magruder, in a hastily written report made the same day of the fight, in which he pleads urgent haste for brevity, takes time to say:

> I cannot speak too highly of the devotion of our troops, all of which did their duty nobly, and whilst it may appear invidious to speak particularly of any regiment or corps when all behaved so well, I am compelled to express my great appreciation of the skill and gallantry of Major Randolph and his Howitzer Battery, and Colonel Hill and the officers and men of the North Carolina Regiment * * * Colonel Hill's determined and judicious action was worthy of his ancient glory.

And in a fuller report, written later, he repeats this at greater length.

Colonel Hill in his report, which is graphic and thrilling as a chapter of romance, says:

> Permit me, in conclusion to pay a well-deserved compliment to the First Regiment North Carolina Volunteers. Their patience under trial, perseverance under toil, and courage under fire have seldom been surpassed by veteran troops. Often working night and day, some times without tents and cooking utensils, a murmur has never escaped them to my knowledge. They have done a large portion of the work on the intrenchments, at Yorktown, as well as those at Bethel. Had all the regiments in the field worked with the same spirit, there would not be an assailable point in Virginia. After the battle they shook hands affectionately with the spades, calling them "clever fellows" and "good friends."
>
> The men are influenced by high moral and religious sentiments, and their conduct has furnished another example of the great truth that he who fears God will ever do his duty to his country.

This is no small praise, coming from that man of few words, who took the performance of duty as a matter of course. The closing words of this unique report are worthy of mention: "Let us devoutly thank the living God for His wonderful interposition in our favor, and evince our gratitude by the exemplariness of our lives."

And the gallant Major Randolph (later our honored Secretary of War), himself without a peer in bravery and skill, reports:

> I am happy in having an opportunity to render my acknowledgments to Colonel Hill, the commandant of the North Carolina regiment, for the useful suggestions which his experience as an artillery officer enabled him to make to me during the action, and to bear testimony to the gallantry and discipline of that portion of his command with which I was associated. The untiring industry of his regiment in intrenching our position enabled us to defeat the enemy with a nominal loss on our side.

Colonel Magruder gives our loss as one killed, and seven wounded. If this is correct, our regiment sustained the entire loss of the day.

Colonel Hill swells the figures to one killed, and eleven wounded, and gives his own casualties as: Private Henry L. Wyatt, Company K, mortally wounded; Lieutenant J.W. Ratchford, contusion; Private Council Rogers, Company H, severely wounded; Private William White, Company K, wounded; Private S. Papperson, Company D, slightly wounded; Private Peter Poteat, Company G, slightly wounded; Private Charles Williams, severely wounded.

Shortly after this victory, Colonel Hill was made a brigadier-general and I was commissioned as his aid-de-camp.

Near the first of October (1861) General Hill was

ordered to North Carolina to take command of the Pamlico line which extended from near Wilmington to the Virginia line, including the defenses of Roanoke Island. At the same time, I received my commission as major and was ordered to report to General Hill.

This commission severed my relations with the First Regiment of North Carolina Volunteers. C. C. Lee succeeded Hill as colonel, and James H. Lane was made lieutenant-colonel. When the six months' enlistment expired, the regiment was disbanded, but all the men went to other regiments, most of them as officers. Out of this regiment came one lieutenant-general, several major-generals, a score or more of brigadier-generals, numerous colonels, and majors, while many promising careers were cut short by death. Among this number was C. C. Lee, who was confidently expected to rise to high rank.

CHAPTER TWO
Friends and Foes
☆　　☆　　☆　　☆

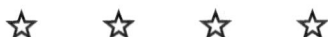

My first realization of the significance of the term *Civil War* came to me early in the war, while listening to Generals D.H. Hill, James Longstreet, and Lafayette Mc-Laws discussing the careers, past and prospective, of their classmates who had graduated with them from West Point in the distinguished class of 1842.

As well as I remember, all but two or three had been accounted for, out of the class of sixty-two members. Many of them had already reached high rank in one or the other of the two armies, and nearly all were destined to play a prominent part in this struggle of one-time friends.

Among those in the Southern Army were Eustis, VanDorn, M.L. Smith, R.H. Anderson, A.P. Stewart, M. Lovell, and G.W. Smith.

These last two had just succeeded in getting into the Confederate lines, after an adventure worthy of mention. At the outbreak of the war they were both street commissioners in New York City. Finding their means of escape practically cut off, they made and carried out a daring plan. Smith, who was a very frail man, fell sick and the doctor (who was probably in the plot), was summoned. He pronounced Smith's condition so serious that no one but Lovell was permitted to see him. He continued to grow worse until he ostensibly died, and a handsome coffin containing bricks was buried with honor, while Smith himself was making his way in disguise, into the Southern lines, where Lovell soon found a way to join him.

Among the Federals mentioned were Newton, who though blind, later obtained renown as the planner and executor of the engineering feat performed for the destruction of Hell Gate in New York harbor, and Sykes who as commander of a regiment of United States regulars, I faced in battle later on several occasions. All had been spoken of in terms of admiration or respect, until Pope's name was mentioned, then there was a chorus of contemptuous exclamations. Some one remarked, "Oh, he'll never amount to any thing; he's too vain and silly for anything except a ball room."

This feeling of contempt was later fruitful of a remark from General Hill that was a by-word in the army while Pope was in command. Just before the Second Battle of Manassas, Pope issued his melodramatic proclamation in which he stated that his headquarters were in the saddle. This came to General Hill's notice, and he gravely remarked, "He was mistaken in his terms; he means his hindquarters."

Rosecrans was mentioned, but no one knew any thing at all of his whereabouts, though it was inferred that he was in the Union Army. General Hill remarked that he dreaded to hear from him as he was a man with a purpose and would make himself felt. We later had reason to realize the truth and correctness of this estimate.

During the four years that followed, many more incidents came under my notice that showed me that this was indeed a civil war – a house divided against itself.

Official Communication With the Enemy and a Postscript to a Friend

The winter of 1861-2, General Hill's command was in winter quarters at Leesburg on the Potomac, and just across the river at Poolsville, was the enemy under General Stone, who had been a messmate and very dear friend of Hill in the Mexican War.

The hostile batteries kept up a constant but ineffectual fire upon each other's camp, until General Hill sent a message under flag of truce, protesting against this useless loss on both sides, as it decided nothing. Several official communications passed between the lines, before it was finally agreed upon that all firing on each other's pickets should cease until one or the other should make a move to cross the river. To one of these official papers, General Hill added a postscript to his old friend Stone. After words of greeting as affectionate as if they were not facing each other in hostile array, he wrote: "I should be glad to have you and your staff come over and breakfast with me, but if you prefer, bring your whole army. In either case you will receive a warm welcome."

To the official reply, General Stone added an answering postscript: "It grieves me to know that my old friend Hill is using his great ability to humiliate the flag under which he learned the art of war, and once so nobly served. I cannot accept your invitation to bring my staff and breakfast with you, but if I should come with my army, I and my brave men will fall with our feet to the foe and our face to the sun, rather than fall into the hands of your master, Jeff Davis, to be treated as the brave Lee and Cogswell." (Lee and Cogswell were Union prisoners held as hostages for the safety of some of our men who were being threatened with death).

As adjutant-general of the department, I carried every flag of truce, and inspected every communication that passed across the lines, and though there was nothing in any of the correspondence unbecoming an officer in Stone's position, it worked much evil to him. He was a Democrat, and hence viewed with suspicion by the powers that were, and when an enemy getting knowledge of his personal relation to Hill, reported it, there was no time lost in taking advantage of the opportunity of ruining him. The room in which he was sleeping with his wife, was entered at 2 o'clock A.M., and he was taken from his bed, like a criminal, and imprisoned at Fort Delaware, where he was kept, without trial, until the end of the war.[1]

Friends as Captors and Prisoners

The night after the first victory at Cold Harbor or

---

1. In a paper published in *Battles and Leaders of the Civil War*, by Richard B. Irwin, Lieut.-Col. and Assistant-Adjutant-General U.S.V., it is stated that Mr. Stanton's order for Stone's arrest was issued on the 28th of January. He further says it was not executed until the 9th of February, and that not only were no charges ever preferred, but no acknowledgment of error was ever made. He was, at the earnest request of General Banks, ordered to report to him in May 1863, and was, after the siege of Port Hudson, appointed chief of his staff, in which capacity he served until April 16, 1864, when under orders previously issued at Washington, he was deprived of his former commission as Brigadier-General, and ordered to report by letter as Colonel of the 14th Infantry. He was again appointed by General Grant as a Brigadier-General in August 1864, and a month later, he resigned.

Gaines' Mill, General Hill, with his brigade commanders, had retired to a house on the battlefield, where he and his officers could have a light, while he gave instructions for the night and the next day. The house had only one room, bare of furniture save for a table and some chairs. Around this table General Hill and his brigadier-generals, R. H. Rhodes, G. B. Anderson, Samuel Garland, and A.H. Colquitt, sat intent on the business in hand, while I dozed in a corner, when suddenly a soldier entered with two prisoners – one a private, the other an officer so badly wounded in the knee that he was supported between his captor and fellow-prisoner. The officer reported to me, and I bade him wait until my superior was at liberty. This entrance had been unnoticed by the men at the table, and as soon as there was a pause in the business I called General Hill's attention to the prisoners. He at once arose and turned toward us. At sight of the wounded man, he sprang forward, and exclaimed regretfully, "Colonel Clitz, you're wounded." Instantly the prisoner loosed his hold on his supporters, and with both hands out stretched, said in a manner very unlike a prisoner reporting to an enemy, "Hill, old fellow, how are you?" There followed such an embrace as is seldom seen between men, and Colonel Clitz was released from General Hill's arms to receive affectionate greeting from General Anderson. Since the time General Hill had first called the prisoner's name, General Garland had been eagerly waiting for a chance to request an introduction. As the introduction was given, the men silently clasped hands, while each seemed shaken by suppressed emotion.

I and others, who had wonderingly watched this little drama, were eager for an explanation of the cause that had turned the report of a prisoner into a friendly reception. General Hill and Colonel Glitz had been tent mates and very dear friends in the Mexican War, and Colonel Glitz was superintendent of West Point while Anderson was a cadet, and by many kindnesses had endeared himself to him. General Garland's young wife, who had died only a few weeks before, had been a ward of Colonel Clitz, and though the men had never met before, this kindred love and grief drew them very close together.

General Hill expressed his regret that no relief could be offered the wounded man, as the surgeons were busy with the wounded of both armies and there was no ambulance to convey him to the field hospital, neither had he any refreshments to offer him. To this apology Colonel Clitz generously replied, "Don't you worry about that, Hill, there are lots of poor fellows who need aid worse than I do." He then told me that his horse had been killed near the house, where he was commanding the United States regulars in the right wing of the army, and that in his holsters I would find a box of cigars and a flask of brandy. I went in search of these things and found the horse, as he said, but some thirsty fellow had found it first, and the pockets were empty. When I reported the failure of my quest, he thanked me and told me that this house had been his own headquarters during the battle, and that he had put a pair of spurs, inlaid with gold, under the edge of the house, at the beginning of the fight, and begged that I would find them and accept them as gift from him. This quest also was unsuccessful.

After a long conversation in which both men seemed to forget that politically they were deadly enemies, General Hill spread his overcoat on the floor, and with that for a bed, they slept like comrades in arms as well as in spirit.

In the morning a hack and driver were secured, and General Hill told Colonel Clitz, that while his duty forced him to send him to Richmond, he would not humiliate him with a guard, and only asked that he report to General Winder at Richmond, where he would receive medical aid. He gave him Mrs. Hill's address and urged that if he needed any aid before he could get into communication with his friends, he apply to her.

Farewells were being said, when a soldier brought in another prisoner of rank, but of most dejected appearance. General Hill at once recognized him as General Reynolds, another comrade of the old army. There was no response to his cordial greeting, only a silent denial of any recognition. Suspecting that the attitude of the prisoner arose from the humiliation at his position, he laid his arm affectionately around his shoulder and said, "Don't feel so badly, Reynolds, all who know you, know you're a good soldier."

The prisoner raised his head instantly, and there was a gleam of pleasure in his eyes as he said, "Do you believe that, Hill? There is no man living whose regard I value more than yours."

And then his passionate self-defense revealed the cause of his humiliation, even before his captor told us that he had been taken asleep, long after sunrise. He said that for four days and nights he had not slept, his command having acted as rear-guard of the army. He had formed his men in position after the rout, and had succumbed to exhaustion, his men had gone off without him, while he slept on as if in a stupor until aroused by the soldier who had taken him prisoner. The offer of aid, which had been made to Colonel Clitz, was in substance, repeated to General Reynolds, and after a friendly farewell they were sent away in the ambulance together.

Hood Charged By His Old Regiment

Early in the same night, while I was trying to gather up some of our division which had been scattered in the pursuit, I came upon General Hood sitting on a cracker-box, crying. His brigade had lost heavily, and all around him were dead and wounded. I spoke to him and he replied brokenly, "Just look here, Major, at these dead and suffering men, and every one of them as good as I am, and yet I am untouched."

A remarkable feature of this fight had been the charge of Federal cavalry against a division of our infantry, and the incident has an added interest from the fact that it was the Fourth Texas Regiment of Infantry, commanded by John B. Hood, that sustained the attack, while it was the Second United States Cavalry in which he had formerly been an officer, that made the charge. This regiment was one of the two created by Jefferson Davis while he was Secretary of War, and the one in which R. E. Lee had formerly been lieutenant-colonel.

At the most desperate moment of the fight, Captain Whiting, who had been Hood's captain on the frontier of Texas, and was now leading the charge, had his horse shot from under him, and fell stunned at the feet of Hood's men and was taken prisoner. About 2 o'clock in the morning, as Hood was going over the field superintending the caring for the wounded and giving orders in his big, unmistakable voice, a man in the dress of a Federal captain, raised himself painfully and asked if that were not Hood. He begged that word be carried to Hood, that his old friend and fellow-soldier in the Second Cavalry, Captain Chambliss, was lying on the battlefield desperately wounded. The word was brought to Hood and he immediately sent a messenger to tell the captain (Chambliss) he would come as soon as possible, and instructed him to give all possible aid to the wounded man. It was not until near daybreak that he was free to go himself to his old friend, and his ministrations until his recovery were as affectionate as if they had not recently joined forces in mortal combat.

Arranging the Cartel for Exchange of Prisoners

Immediately following the fights around Richmond in 1862, General D. H. Hill, of the Confederate Army, and General Jno. A. Dix, of the Federal Army, were chosen by their respective governments to arrange a cartel for the exchange of prisoners.

General Hill requested his staff to accompany him, and several of them spent all their money and much pains to provide refreshments that would impress the company they were to meet.

At the time appointed, General Hill with all his staff except Lieutenant Reid and myself, whose uniforms we considered too shabby to grace such an occasion, had been granted permission to remain in camp, left for Haxall's Landing on the James River, where the meeting was to take place. There they were met by General Dix and his entire staff, who had come up the river in a boat. The first day, General Hill and his party were entertained by General Dix on board the boat, where lavish entertainment had been carefully prepared. Both generals were careful abstainers, but not so all the men. The drinking was kept up throughout the afternoon, while the principals were busy over the business in hand, and when the time came to separate for the night, most of them were "gentlemanly tight."

The next day, General Dix and his party were General Hill's guests and the business was taken up again, while the men set themselves to consuming the refreshments so painstakingly prepared, and the guests were loud in their praise of the liquor, which they wonderingly pronounced better than anything in the government stores. And when the time came to part, the condition of the day before prevailed.

The principals had now gone as far as their instructions authorized them, and each went back to his own headquarters.

A few days later, having received further instructions, they met again. This time General Hill bade Lieutenant Reid and I to accompany him, and with only the three in the party we set out. At Haxall Landing, we were met by General Dix with only two then, neither of whom had been of the other party. The two generals exchanged amused smiles of understanding as each viewed the scanty train of the other.

While they were at work, I fell into a conversation with one of the men, an officer of General McClellan's staff. In a friendly way, we exchanged experiences, and discussed the part of the war we had seen. He cheerfully admitted that, up to that time, we had the best of them, but assured me that their time would come. In the course of the conversation, he told me that in the fight at Gaines' Mill, an entire regiment of Union infantry, with the exception of one man, was killed or severely wounded by one volley of bullets. The incident had caused a good deal of speculation among the Federals. He asked me if I knew anything of it. This interested me greatly, as it coincided with a story told me by Colonel Jenkins only a few days before. He commanded the Fifth South Carolina Infantry, probably at that time the best drilled regiment in the Confederate service. The men were of superior character, and Colonel Jenkins himself was a very efficient officer. He came of one of the old aristocratic families of South Carolina, and was a man of high ideals.

I had not doubted his veracity in the narrative, but I had felt sure he was in some way mistaken in the facts, until this man's story corroborated all he had said.

At one point in the fight, Colonel Jenkins' command was advancing to the attack of a Union regiment that was on its knees, with rifles raised, ready to receive them. He had given strict orders that they were to march deliberately, ready to swing their guns into position at his word, but on no account to discharge a shot until he commanded. It would have been a great risk to put an ordinary regiment to such a test, but the excellent character and discipline of his men made it possible. They continued to advance toward the waiting enemy, until Colonel Jenkins heard the first sound of the enemy's command, "Ready, aim, fire." And before the "Ready" was said, he had given the sharp order, "Fire!" His command was so well obeyed, that not an answering shot came back.

A Prisoner Who Proved a White Elephant

While our army was fighting Rosecrans in Georgia, we took a prisoner who proved pretty much of a white elephant on our hands.

Doctor Mary Walker, who was an assistant surgeon in the Federal Army, presuming on her connection with the medical fraternity and on her sex, rode boldly up to our picket, and asked if he would take some letters which she wished delivered in our lines. The soldier very gallantly replied that he would take them and her too. She was indignant, and protested vigorously against being taken prisoner. Her indignation was still in evidence when she was brought into camp, and her protestation was repeated to General Hill, who was very much amused, and told her that she was probably giving him as much trouble as he was giving her, as he could neither keep her nor turn her loose. He sent her to General Bragg, and he sent her to Richmond, where she was shortly paroled or exchanged.

Her appearance excited a good deal of curiosity in our camp, as she was the first American woman to publicly wear bloomers, yet her patent leather boots, and plumed hat gave her a very dainty appearance, though she was not at all pretty, she was far from being ugly. In recent years, I have read several magazine articles about this woman and her work, and still more written by her, and I always think of her as she was referred to in our camps – as "The White Elephant." And I mean no disrespect to her.

CHAPTER THREE
Some Famous Men of the Confederacy
☆　☆　☆　☆

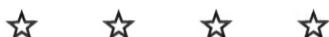

During my service at different times in the Army of Northern Virginia, and the Army of Tennessee, it was my good fortune to come in contact with most of the famous men of the Southern Army, and I have many cherished memories of their kindliness, humor, eccentricities, and other personal traits that are not often reflected from the pages of history.

Mr. Davis and His Cabinet

I had seen Mr. Davis several times before I had the honor of being known to him. Late in the spring of 1862, General Hill took me with him to Mr. Davis' house. It was about 10 o'clock in the morning when we called, and we were informed, to our surprise, that the President was still in bed, but he sent word that he would see us immediately. When he came into the room, I was startled at his thin appearance and his air of suffering. In apology for being in bed so late, he said he had been suffering from indigestion. His manner was very courteous, and during the course of the call he offered us some cigars, which were the strongest, blackest I had ever seen.

General Hill after smoking his for a few minutes, remarked to Mr. Davis that it was a wonder he did not suffer from a worse ailment than indigestion if he was in the habit of smoking such cigars as that.

I saw him again late in June, on the first day of the Seven Days' Battles around Richmond. He had ridden some six or seven miles out from Richmond on the Mechanicsville pike to a ford on the Chickahominy, from which A.P. Hill had just driven the enemy. He with R.E. Lee and several others, was watering his horse in the ford as I came by carrying an important message. Thinking only of the urgency of our mission, I hardly noticed the men, and without checking the speed of my horse, I dashed into the river, which was some two or three feet deep, splashing water on all the men and nearly knocking Mr. Davis' horse off his feet. There was no time for apologies even if I had thought of making any.

Later in the day, when I spoke regretfully of the incident, Lieutenant West said, "That ends your promotion, you're a finished number." Whether or not this incident had any influence in determining my future rank, the prophecy proved very nearly true. Though I was repeatedly recommended for promotion by some of the ablest men in the army, my next commission was not issued until so late in the war that it never reached me. If Mr. Davis remembered the incident, he probably thought so heedless a person as I had appeared to be was not a safe subject for promotion.

He remembered me and was very courteous when I met him again in July of 1863, when he came out from Richmond to meet General Hill, who by skilful generalship, had just driven back the enemy under General Schofield, who was advancing on Richmond from Fortress

Monroe. He expressed in high terms his appreciation of the country's indebtedness to General Hill, and made him lieutenant-general on the field.

I saw him again in October of the same year, when he came to Missionary Ridge to learn why General Bragg had not followed up the victory of Chickamauga. He brought General Pemberton with him to take the place of General Polk, who had been falsely accused by Bragg of disobedience of orders during the battle, and who was then under arrest. This was the first of a series of charges brought by Bragg against able men in his effort to cover his own cowardice and incompetency in this campaign. The council of Bragg and his generals, which Mr. Davis called for the purpose of learning the true state of affairs, is worthy of longer mention than can be given it here.

I saw him again while he was visiting the Army of Tennessee, under General Hood at Lovejoy Station in Georgia. I saw him bid General Hood good-bye and God-speed, as he mounted his horse to follow his army, which had already begun its march to Nashville. We all understood this as orders to General Hood from the President to fight.

I saw him for the last time in Greensboro, N. C., after Lee had surrendered, and while Johnston was negotiating with Sherman for the surrender of our army.

Mr. Davis was a type of the old Southern aristocracy, whose culture, intellect, and virtue had so large a part in forming the Union and building up its strength, and resources, which made our defeat possible. His fault, if we can bring ourselves to speak of faults in one who has been made to be the scapegoat for the sins and mistakes of many, was his blind belief in the ability of men, who were unfitted for the high places to which he called them, and his determination to make heroes of them in spite of the abundant evidence they gave that they were not of the hero-stuff.

Of four men, Walker, Benjamin, Randolph, and Breckenridge, who successively served as Secretary of War of the Confederacy, I had the pleasure of knowing the last three. I knew Walker, who was the provisional Secretary, only in a general way, but was on familiar terms with Benjamin, a Jew, who had been United States Senator from Louisiana before the war, and at the time of Virginia's secession, was a lawyer in Richmond. In physical appearance he was a familiar type of his nation, low and heavy-set. After his services as Secretary of War, he was made Secretary of State. When the war ended, being one of the men proscribed by the United States Government, he fled to England, where he soon rose to prominence as a member of the judiciary, and at the time of his death, was one of the highest judicial officers of the kingdom.

Somewhat similar is the story of Quartermaster Myers, another Jew, of Mr. Davis' Cabinet. When the war broke out, he was quartermaster of the Texas division of the United States Army. When it closed, he escaped to Germany, where his kindred were people of prominence and wealth. After I came to Texas, I had some correspondence with him, which indicated that during the closing years of his life, he enjoyed an unusual degree of prosperity and happiness.

My acquaintance with General Randolph, who succeeded Benjamin as Secretary of War, began at the very first of the war, when he commanded the Battalion of Richmond Howitzers. As his name indicates, he came of Virginia's highest aristocracy, and was in all respects an honor to his family. Before he was called to the Cabinet, he had risen to the rank of General of Artillery, but he was always known among his men and brother officers as "The Young Lieutenant," a title he had gained in the United States Navy, where he had gained widespread distinction from an incident which occurred on the coast of Northern Africa.

There had been some discussion with the officers of a British ship over the results of the Revolutionary War, and the War of 1812. One of the Englishmen had made a remark insulting to the dignity of our nation, and Randolph, then only a midshipman, challenged him to a duel. The duel was fought, and the Englishman wounded, but not seriously, while Randolph was unhurt.

Prominent in my memory of great men, there stands John C. Breckenridge, whose physique, I believe, was the most perfect I have ever seen. His very physical appearance was enough to justify the idolatry accorded him by the Southern Democracy. I had admired him greatly while he was Vice-President under Buchanan, and though I was too young to vote, I gave my loudest cheer for him in the Presidential election, which resulted in placing Lincoln in the White House.

I had admired him from afar so long, that it was a great pleasure to meet him when I went with General Hill to the Army of Tennessee, where he went to take command of a corps, in which Breckenridge was a division commander. I saw him in the fight at Chickamauga, where his bearing was all my admiration could desire. I cannot speak of his behavior in higher terms than to say he suffered none in comparison with the gallant Cleburne, who commanded the other division of the corps. He was never held in high favor by Bragg who possessed the faculty of alienating every able man with whom he came in contact, except Mr. Davis, who maintained a high regard for him to the end of the war, in spite of his ignorance and incapability.

My duty as adjutant-general of the corps, often brought me in contact with General Cooper, Adjutant-General of the Confederacy. He always persisted in treating me in a kindly, paternal way that offended my dignity. Once I was sent with a message to him from General Hill, and not finding him at his office, I went to his home, where I had been told he had gone for some needed rest. Mrs. Cooper told me the general was resting, but if my message was urgent, she would rouse him. I thought it was, and the general was called, and he came down in a very gruff humor. He scolded me soundly for disturbing him, and said General Hill should know that he had to have some rest. His words seemed to act as a safety valve for his wrath, and he was soon his usual kindly self. Mrs. Cooper, wishing to remove any sting I might feel from her husband's words, brought out refreshments of cake and wine, and was very gracious every way. I was later the recipient of another scolding from the same source.

In accordance with orders, I reported to him for assignment to duty after I had been relieved from the Army of Tennessee with General Hill, who was the third victim of Bragg's attempt to clear himself in the eyes of the public. At my appearance, his wrath again burst bonds, and he demanded to know my reasons for being absent from my command. I showed him my orders, and explained my presence. Then his wrath was turned in another direction, and I had the pleasure of hearing him express in part my own feeling toward Bragg, who, he said, had overstepped his authority. He ended by sending me back to my command to remain there until he should relieve me or, as he jestingly added, I should be relieved by a court-martial, as that was the only authority besides himself that could relieve me.

Robert E. Lee

I had often seen General Lee around Richmond, and may have met him, but I had no particular interest in him until he came to the Army of Northern Virginia, immediately after the Battle of Seven Pines, to succeed General Joseph E. Johnston, who had been severely wounded in that battle. He made an impressive figure as he rode down the line. I judge that at this time he was some fifty-two or fifty-three years old. His hair and beard were an iron-gray, and gave an added dignity to his military bearing. I had a closer view of him next day when I went with General Hill to his headquarters. His features were intelligent and kindly and inspired immediate confidence in his high ideals and devotion to duty, and yet there was an air of sternness about him. I remember having the impression that here was a man who got the truth from all with whom he came in contact, for no one would dare try to deceive him.

Viewing Robert E. Lee from all standpoints, I consider him the greatest man the war produced either North or South (I say this, in the beginning lest some things I say may be misunderstood), yet I know some others that I think excelled him in some points. I consider Joseph E. Johnston his equal, if not his superior, as a military commander.

If Lee had time to plan a battle, and could make a fight on his own plan, victory was certain, but he lacked the faculty, which Johnston possessed, of adapting his plans to changes in those of the enemy, and of beating them at their own game. Though he at all times had the love and loyalty of the whole army, he did not possess such a magnetic personality as that of Johnston, which was felt even to the lowest private, and made him eager for a fight if Johnston led, certain that the end would be victory for them.

My own thoughts of Lee in battle were almost those of indifference. I knew he had a good plan which, if nothing went wrong, would be successful, but as this was improbable, my confidence of victory was in his under officers. This impression may have been due to an incident that occurred while we were returning from the Maryland campaign.

After lying all day on the battlefield after the Sharpsburg fight, we crossed the Potomac, and went into camp about a mile from the river. The reserve artillery of the army crossed later, and stopped on the south bank of the river, under a bluff, where it was left without the protection of infantry. The enemy on discovering our retreat, had followed us with a large body of cavalry. Over a thousand of these crossed the river and captured the reserve artillery of the army.

That night after we had gone into camp, General Lee issued an order to march, which directed General Hill to follow General Jackson. About sunrise next morning, General Hill at the head of his division, reported to General Lee and asked for orders. We found him pacing restlessly before his tent and showing great agitation. His reply to General Hill's request was, "Follow Jackson," and there was no further information. General Hill asked which road Jackson had taken. General Lee's reply was that he did not know. He then told us that a courier had brought a report of the capture of his reserve artillery, but that this report had been denied, and he was anxiously waiting the return of the messenger he had sent to learn the truth. He seemed to me to be very much troubled and undecided as to what course to pursue. General Hill waited a few minutes, and again asked for orders, and received the same answer, "Follow Jackson."

General Hill knew his silent brother-in-law so well that this reply was not quite so enigmatical as it seemed. He at once started his division on a double quick march for the river. When we had gone about one-half the distance, we heard the report of heavy firing which told us that something was happening. As General Hill had surmised, General Jackson had heard the report of the captured artillery after he had started on his march, and had gone back to the river. He was now firing from the bluff on the enemy, who were in possession of our artillery. The result was the recapture of the artillery, the almost complete destruction of the enemy's cavalry, which had crossed the river, and very little loss to us.

Late in November, 1862, General Hill was ordered by General Lee to move his headquarters from Winchester, Virginia, to Fredericksburg, where the army was being concentrated. In spite of bad roads and the worst of weather, General Hill with more than eight thousand men, made this march over the Blue Ridge Mountains in ten days without the loss of a man unaccounted for.

When we reached Fredericksburg, I was sent to report the arrival of the division to General Lee. He asked me a great many questions about the condition of our division, especially as to straggling. I reported that it was never better, and that we had arrived with every man we started with, except those accounted for.

He seemed very much gratified by the report, but still seemed doubtful about the accuracy of my report concerning the stragglers, and asked me what means General Hill had taken to prevent straggling. I told him that every officer in the division, even down to the sergeants, were held responsible for the men in their charge. I think he still felt a slight uncertainty about this, until General Hill's report, and his own inspection of the troops, verified my statement. And indeed, under the circumstances, it did seem impossible.

I saw him daily, but did not come in contact with him until the Tuesday afternoon after the Battle of Fredericksburg on Sunday.

I was sitting on a redoubt on our line of battle with a field glass watching the movements of the enemy. Seeing that I had a field glass, he stopped his horse in front of me, and asked what I saw. I told him the enemy seemed to be crossing the river. He replied that I was mistaken, that the big fight would come off next day. I learned that his assertion was based on a captured message from General Burnside, which gave him knowledge of the intended attack the day after the battle. This plan had been abandoned, and the next day found the enemy across the river as I had thought.

Soon after this incident, I was ordered to North Carolina, and thence to the Army of Tennessee, thus missing the pleasure of participating in some of his most brilliant movements which followed.

Joseph E. Johnston

I saw Joseph E. Johnston for the first time, in Centreville, Virginia, when General D.H. Hill reported to him for duty in the Army of Northern Virginia, of which he was then in command. I have never met any one whose personality so impressed me at the first meeting. He looked every inch the soldier that he was, and impressed me as a man of keen perception and quick actions, one who would be equal to all occasions. I soon found this was the universal opinion of the army, and the men had the utmost confidence that he knew what he was doing, and would be ready to meet every emergency.

I saw him again in the spring of 1862, at Yorktown, and on May 5th, I saw him at the Battle of Williamsburg. He was at Fort Magruder directing the battle, and as report after report came in from different parts of the fight, he seemed not to be in the least excited or worried. No move of the enemy seemed to surprise him, without seeming hesitation he gave orders as confidently as if checking names off a list.

McClellan's army was in such overwhelming numbers that we found it necessary to retreat that night and all the next day. The country was flooded from recent heavy rains, and frequently the wheels of the artillery and wagons would be dragging their axles in the mud. When we went into camp after this march of more than eighteen hours, the hindmost troops were only six miles from the field of battle. Yet there was no grumbling among the soldiers and we lost not a single wagon nor a piece of artillery.

One evening, while on this march from Williamsburg, I was sent by General Hill to headquarters with a written message for General Johnston. Staff officers ordinarily carried only verbal messages, written ones being sent by courier. I wore no badge of rank, and General Johnston, not recognizing me, ordered me to report to a sergeant and wait his time to formulate a reply. This was in the presence of his own and General G. W. Smith's staff, all of whom recognized me and raised a laugh at my discomfiture. Colonel S. W. Melton, a man from my own town, but a much older man than I, enjoyed my embarrassment for a moment and then introduced me as General Hill's adjutant-general. General Johnston was very careful of the observances of military etiquette, and he apologized for not recognizing me. He then invited me to be seated on the gallery, where the other officers were gathered. Early in the war, not half the officers in our army wore uniforms. General Magruder still wore his buff trousers and blue coat. I had had none since my cadet uniform had worn out, but this incident determined me to get one some way. When we reached Richmond I went to a tailor, and asked him to let me have a major's uniform. He assured me that he had just what I wanted in my size, and sold me a conglomerated outfit that bore more resemblance to a Federal surgeon's uniform than any thing else I have ever seen. I accepted this, thinking it full uniform, and wore it with all pride until one day I rode to General Smith's headquarters, and Colonel Melton called out to know when I had become a Yankee surgeon. When I found out my blunder, my mortification knew no bounds. I saw General Johnston wounded in the Battle of Seven Pines, while directing the fight in person.

General Hill, who had seen him in several fights in the Mexican War, remarked that it did not surprise him at all, as Johnston was almost certain to be hit in every fight into which he went. He told me of one occasion in the Mexican War when Johnston, then an engineer, was hit while reconnoitering, and he was put in his place, and compelled to use the field glasses still warm with Johnston's blood.

The wound Johnston received in this fight was of so serious a nature that General Lee was put in command of this army and I never saw him again until he came to the Army of Tennessee in 1863, while we were in winter quarters at Dalton, Georgia. The army was in a very poor condition as a result of the Battle of Missionary Ridge and the long mismanagement of Bragg. The men were low-spirited, had lost all enthusiasm, and felt as if they were already beaten.

General Johnston, not wishing to harass the men unnecessarily by a general review, made it known that he would inspect each brigade separately and on its own ground. Our corps was the first to be inspected, and General Johnston invited General Hindman, who then commanded the corps, to ride with him. He, with all his staff and about a dozen men, and two White servants, called at General Johnston's headquarters, where we found him waiting for us without an officer or attendant. As he mounted his beautiful little thoroughbred mare, which had been presented to him by the citizens of Richmond, and rode unattended, except for his military bearing and air of distinction, it would have seemed that he was the inferior officer, and General Hindman the commander of the army.

I rode ahead and formed the brigade in line, and when General Johnston came up, I felt a sense of pity for the discouragement he must feel at this first outlook, for a more forlorn, dejected, hopeless looking set of men I have never seen. There was silence as he rode down the line, and as he came back to the starting point in the rear, one poor fellow screwed up courage enough to give one solitary cheer. In response to this, General Johnston rode to the front, wheeled his nimble little mare about and raised his cap. Instantly there was a cheer from every man in the brigade; life and hope seemed to come back, and thus it remained while Johnston commanded the army. I was told that this was typical of his reception throughout the army.

He was everywhere in evidence during the campaign from Dalton to Atlanta, covering seventy-five days, during which time the Battles of Resaca, Calhoun, Alleyton, Cassville, New Hope Church, Henrietta, and Kenesaw Mountain, besides numerous skirmishes, were fought. Although there was rain almost every day, the roads were bad, and all physical comforts were lacking, the men never lost confidence in their commander. They were often heard to say, as Johnston rode by, "There goes old Joe; he don't look like he's whipped, and I ain't till he is."

Shortly after we reached Atlanta, Johnston was relieved from command of the army (July 17, 1864). This proved to be one of the saddest blunders Mr. Davis made during his whole term of office, and was so considered throughout the army at the time. The reason given by Mr. Davis for this act was that Johnston was not fighting enough, while statistics show that the battles named above, besides numerous skirmishes were fought, and that on that march our army lost nine thousand men, while Sherman lost fifty thousand.

After he was relieved from command, I saw him no more until just before the fight at Bentonville, N.C., when he was put in command of all the troops not under General Lee, consisting of the remnant of the Army of Tennessee, the troops from Charleston and those from Wilmington. The fact that he accepted this command, is a better commentary on the nobility of his nature than any

I can make. Bragg was given the command of the troops from Wilmington, and Hardee that of those from Charleston, but before the arrival of either Johnston or Bragg, General D. H. Hill was the ranking officer of the army. As it was known throughout the army, that Bragg had used his great influence with the President to humiliate both Johnston and Hill, an altogether harmonious state of affairs was not to be expected, and while General Johnston was still in Greensboro, he sent a telegram to General Hill, to the effect that Bragg would soon be there and would outrank him. "But," he added, "I know your patriotism and generosity too well to suppose this will make any difference in the discharge of your duty, but I will come down in a few days, and relieve you of all embarrassment." He came in time to command all troops in the Bentonville fight.

After this battle, our army was marched to Greensboro, and on the way we heard the news of General Lee's surrender, and the evacuation of Richmond. Johnston sent a flag of truce to Sherman, and asked an interview with him. It was granted, and they met at Goldsborough. When he returned, General S. D. Lee and a part of his staff, who had been at the front of the line, met him. He told us that he had agreed to surrender the army, and showed us a copy of the agreement. General S. D. Lee read them aloud, and as he did so the tears which had been gathering in Johnston's eyes burst bounds and trickled down his cheeks.

These agreements could have no binding force until they should be approved by both Mr. Lincoln and Mr. Davis. They were so liberal that General Lee asked General Johnston if he supposed Mr. Lincoln would approve them. Johnston replied that he had asked General

Sherman the same question, and he had told him that they were the terms which he had been authorized by Mr. Lincoln to make, and then he said he would prove that he was acting in good faith. He called his adjutant-general in, and in Johnston's presence, directed that all the heavy artillery of the army be at once sent on its way to Newberne where it would be loaded on board ship. He then dictated a message to Washington that transportation for all his army be sent at once to Newberne. And before Johnston left his headquarters he had given a copy of the terms to an officer with directions to take it to Mr. Lincoln and get it approved as soon as possible. The messenger arrived in Washington the night that Lincoln was assassinated, and in the morning, when Andrew Johnson had been sworn into office, the terms of agreement were submitted to him, but instead of approving them, he wrote on the back, "We make no terms with rebels; an unconditional surrender or nothing."

On the return of the messenger, Sherman declared the armistice at an end, and announced that aggressive movements would begin at noon next day.

By this time many of our men, to escape surrender, had deserted, and were making their way to the Trans-Mississippi Department, where they hoped the war would be continued. There seemed to be nothing for Johnston to do but ask for another conference, the result of which was the surrender of our army upon the same terms as Grant had given Lee.

Johnston's copy of the first agreement was among the papers, that I, as his adjutant-general surrendered, but I have an official copy of these and an accurate copy may be found in *Johnston's Narrative*.

During the trying time while the details of the sur-

render were being arranged, the love and loyalty and devotion which the men still felt for their old commander,
were expressed by their prolonged cheers when ever he
appeared.

Lieutenant-General S. D. Lee

There are many incidents in the military career of
Lieutenant-General Stephen D. Lee, that make it, perhaps, the most distinguished of any in the Southern Army.
He held more different ranks than any other man in our
army, and was the only man I ever knew who gained distinction as an officer in all three departments of the land
forces: artillery, cavalry, and infantry.

He was a native of my own State, South Carolina,
where his family was a distinguished one. He had graduated from West Point, and had reached the rank of First
Lieutenant in the United States Army, when he resigned
to enter the Confederate service. He was at once made an
officer on General Beauregard's staff, and carried the
order from General Beauregard to the battery that fired
the first shot on Fort Sumter. A short time afterwards he
was made captain of the battery of Hampton's Legion,
later noted as the famous Hart's Battery, with the cavalry
of the Army of Northern Virginia. His command went to
Virginia early in the war, and he retained the position
there for nearly a year. It was here I first met him, Major
James F. Hart, who was then his first lieutenant, being my
brother-in-law. He was next made major of artillery, then
lieutenant-colonel of cavalry, and then colonel of artillery,
and given command of a regiment of artillery which he
commanded in the Second Battle of Manassas. It is said
that never, in the history of war, had one man commanded so much artillery, with so much skill and effect as

he did here.

This secured his promotion to brigadier-general, and he was sent to Vicksburg, where he greatly distinguished himself. He surrendered at the fall of this place, but was paroled soon afterwards, and was made a major-general of cavalry, and assigned to the command of Mississippi, where General Forrest was operating. For his services here, he was made lieutenant-general. Forrest, also a brigadier-general, sent a message of congratulation on his promotion, and in reply Lee protested that the War Department had made a mistake, and that it was Forrest who should have had the promotion.

He was sent to the Army of Tennessee to take command of Hood's corps, when Hood was promoted to succeed Johnston in command of the army. It was then, as adjutant-general of this corps, that my most intimate relations with him began. It did not take us long to realize that he was a man of unusual ability, and we rejoiced in the good fortune that had sent us so able a commander in place of the devoutly admired Hood.

He took command on the 27th of July. The next day, and again on the 31st, he with his corps, opposed Sherman's flank movement around Atlanta. The skill he showed in handling the troops, his personal courage, and many other admirable traits of character, soon endeared him to the men of the corps.

I was closely associated with him on the campaign with Hood to Nashville. When we came to the Tennessee River, opposite Florence, Alabama, his corps was the first to cross the river in small boats and attack the enemy, who were driven out.

There were more pretty girls here than I have ever seen in any one town. We were hospitably entertained by the people, and during our ten days' stay, General Lee, who was then unmarried, like several of the staff, was not at all indifferent to the charms of the beautiful girls.

We moved from Florence to Columbia, Tennessee, which was occupied by the Federals. It was arranged that an attack was to be made at daylight the next day. General Lee's corps was put in front; with skirmishers out and cavalry ahead, we started a little before daylight, but soon discovered that the enemy had vacated the place. Our entrance into the city is one of the things I shall never forget, and shall speak of it in connection with General Forrest.

Our corps was left in Columbia, while Hood was off on a Jacksonian march, which, if his orders had been obeyed, would in all human probability have been a success, and would have resulted in the capture or destruction of Thomas' army. General Lee succeeded so well in deceiving the Federal army across the river, that for a whole day they thought Hood was still in the city. It was here that Colonel Beckham, chief of our artillery, was mortally wounded.

The next day we fought the Battle of Franklin, in which we lost twenty-seven general officers, killed and wounded. Among the killed was the gallant General Pat Cleburne. The enemy evacuated that night, and we followed them on into sight of Nashville. During all the fighting around Nashville, Lee's line never wavered, until the line in another part of the army broke, and the enemy were about to get into our rear. The morning after the rout of the army, a part of Lee's corps were the only organized troops in the whole army.

We crossed the river at Franklin the next day, and were followed by Federal cavalry. Shortly after we got across, a heavy volley of shot were fired at us. General Lee was wounded in the foot while spurring his horse. The enemy were driven back, and but two men knew General Lee had been hit, until we had gone some two or three miles further on, when the pain had become so intense that he had to have his boot cut off, and the ball extracted. It was found that several bones were broken, but he stayed with the army until he was threatened with lockjaw, and he was forced to ask for a furlough. He was able to return to the army on crutches only in time to surrender with Johnston. During his convalescence, he had married Miss Harrison, of Mississippi, to whom he had been engaged for a long time.

At the time of the surrender, he was only thirty-three years of age, and had held every rank in the army from cadet at West Point to lieutenant-general. It has been my pleasure to meet him several times since the war, and the meeting with him is for me, the most pleasant feature of the general reunions of the United Confederate Veterans, of which he is now commander-in-chief.[1]

Stonewall Jackson

The beginning of my personal acquaintance with General Jackson is so merged with what I knew of him before, that I am uncertain just where it began. I was honored with the confidence of General D. H. Hill, who was so closely connected with General Jackson, that I knew, perhaps, more of that strange man's plans, and traits of

---

1. The above was written in the fall of 1907, when General Lee was in good health, but has since been called to join the other great commanders of our dead Confederacy. His death occurred in May, 1908.

character that are concerned with his inner self than any officer of his own staff.

I am quite sure I did not see him during the first year of the war. In the winter of 1861-2, he had his command in winter quarters in the Valley of Virginia, across the mountains from us. It was while here that an incident occurred which came near depriving the Confederacy of his valuable services. His men were greatly in need of blankets, overcoats, and other winter supplies, and knowing that General Banks, who was just across the river, had received a bountiful supply of these things, he took some of his picked troops, crossed over in the dead of night, and so routed the Federals that he was able to return with a valuable supply of the much-needed articles. One of his officers, irritated by his uncommunicativeness and silence in regard to his intended movements, complained to the War Department. As a result of this complaint, Secretary of War Benjamin reprimanded Jackson for disturbing his men while they were in winter quarters. General Jackson replied that it seemed to him improbable that a civilian, two hundred miles from the scene of action, should know more of the details of the command of the army than the commander on the field, and he therewith tendered his resignation. Mr. Davis considered this an act of insubordination, and was about to accept the resignation, when the news got abroad, and such was the pressure brought to bear, that the President thought best not to disregard it, and the resignation was refused.

Just before the fights around Richmond, when Jackson was known to be in the Valley with his own and Ewell's divisions, General D. H. Hill was so anxious to know of his brother-in-law's movements, that he sent me to Richmond every day to see the dispatches on the bulletin-board. One day I found this very unique dispatch: "By the blessing of God we have gained a victory over Banks. Send me more troops and no orders. (Signed) T. J. Jackson, Major-General." Several days later I found a similar dispatch: "By the blessing of God we have gained a victory over Fremont. Send me more troops and no orders." It was signed as before. And the next day I found a dispatch which I should have known to be Jackson's without the signature. It was a repetition of the others except for the name of the defeated general. This time it was, "By the blessing of God we have gained a victory over Shields. Send me more troops and no orders."

Soon after this, about the middle of June, General Hill came back to his camp from the council of war at General Lee's headquarters, where the plan for turning McClellan's right was consummated. He told me that General Jackson was present at this council, having ridden horseback from Gordonsville, a distance of over seventy miles, in less than twenty hours. And on the 27th of June, Jackson appeared on Lee's left in time to take part in the Battle of Cold Harbor or Gaines' Mill.

In his brilliant campaign in the Valley, with only twenty thousand men, he had virtually destroyed the armies of Banks, Fremont, and Shields, an aggregate of seventy-five thousand men, and had so alarmed the authorities at Washington that they had recalled McDowell, thus lessening the fighting force of McClellan by thirty thousand men, and while they were expecting Jackson to knock at the gates of the city, he was back in Virginia helping Lee.

I think it was during these fights that I first met General Jackson, and I next saw him at Fredericksburg while Lee was preparing to fight Burnside, and during the battle when he commanded the right wing of Lee's army. Later, when the army was in winter quarters, I saw him often, for he and General Hill made frequent visits to each other, and I was present at many of these visits. During this time I saw many evidences of his deep piety and reverence for the Sabbath. He had, in common with General Hill, the habit of holding a sort of family prayers with his staff and any other soldiers who cared to come when possible. His Presbyterian teaching was so much a part of him that it seemed impossible to startle him, and no persuasion could turn him aside from what he thought his duty. Though he did not hesitate to attend to public business when duty demanded it, he ever personally kept the Sabbath holy. In it no business of a private nature was transacted, and even a letter from his wife, coming on Sunday, would be left unopened until the Sabbath was over.

One Sunday I rode with Major Avery, who was a brother-in-law to Jackson, to his headquarters where he presented an application for a furlough for himself, which had been made out and signed by General Hill the day before. He explained what it was and asked Jackson's signature, and in turn was asked if it was anything urgent. On being told that it was not, General Jackson put it in a pigeon-hole, and said, "I'll attend to it to-morrow."

While the army was on its march up the Valley, I saw an instance of his strict insistence upon prompt obedience to orders. On this occasion he had ordered General A.P. Hill to move with his division at sunrise. Some little time after sunrise, he rode by, and found the division ready for marching, but waiting for A.P. Hill to come up and give the order to start. Jackson himself gave the order, and joined D.H. Hill at the head of his division. A few minutes later, A.P. Hill came dashing up, and extended his sword to General Jackson, saying, "General Jackson, if you are going to command my division, you had better take my sword." Without any note of unusual excitement or sternness in his voice, General Jackson replied, "Put up your, sword, General Hill, and take your place at the rear of your division." Then turning to a staff officer he said, "Tell General Branch to take command of General A.P. Hill's division." This ended the controversy, and in a few days General Hill was restored to his command.

Jackson's character is a very hard one to analyze. Any one who came much in contact with him, felt many fine shades of character that cannot well be defined. But there were some elements in his nature that no one, with even a slight acquaintance with him, could fail to recognize, such as his devotion to duty, his beautiful piety, and his strong determination. Under a stolid seeming, rather uncouth exterior, he had a nature as fine in its perceptions and sympathies as a woman's.

He had a fine, but not brilliant, mind that made up for his slowness in acquiring knowledge, by his fidelity in retaining it, and its absolute accuracy. He had a hold on the affections of his troops that I have never seen equaled. Whenever he appeared among his troops, there was a proud, affectionate cheering which continued as he was in sight. It came to be a common saying among the troops whenever distant cheering was heard, "They see Old Stonewall or a rabbit."

After his old gray uniform and cap had become very dingy, General Jeb. Stuart presented him with a fine new uniform including cap and overcoat. The first time he appeared in them among the men, he was not immediately recognized, and there was silence until some one shouted,

"Come out of them Jackson, you can't fool us," and the cheering began as of old.

General John B. Hood

My acquaintance with General Hood began very early in the war, when as first lieutenant of the regular army of the Confederacy, he reported for service to General D. H. Hill, who commanded the Department of the Peninsula, with headquarters at Yorktown, Virginia. At that time there were some half-dozen companies of cavalry scattered over the Peninsula with no more compact organization than that of a company. General Hill assigned Lieutenant Hood to the command of all the cavalry in the Peninsula, and, in the order of assignment, called him Major Hood, to prevent any possible discontent on the part of the company captains, all of whom outranked him. This deception worked well, and he soon had the cavalry of the Peninsula under good organization with a complete system of pickets and espionage.

In this position I left him the last of September, and saw him no more until I met him again in Yorktown in the spring of 1862, when he held the rank of brigadier-general in Johnston's army, and commanded his famous Texas brigade. From that time on, to the spring of 1863, I saw him frequently, at the Williamsburg fight, on Johnston's march to the vicinity of Richmond, at the Battle of Seven Pines, the Seven Days' Battles around Richmond, at Gaines' Mill, and at Savage Station, and at all of these places his command did such valiant service that Hood's Brigade came to be felt as a power in the army. The fight at Cedar Mountain, the Second Battle of Manassas, the Battle of South Mountain, and the Battle of Sharpsburg, so enhanced the fame of the Texas brigade and its commander that its very name was worth more in battle than two such brigades could have been without their well-deserved reputation. Few generals have possessed the warm personal love of their men as Hood did. This attachment was something different from any feeling I have ever known to exist between men and commander; there was more of an element of comradeship in it. I saw an evidence of the devotion of the brigade to its commander just before the Battle of Boonesborough, in Maryland. Hood's Brigade had been temporarily joined to Evans' Brigade with General Evans in command of the whole. For some trivial excuse General Evans had ordered Hood under arrest. While the brigade was going from Boonesborough to South Mountain to go into the fight with Hood riding at the rear under arrest, they met General R. E. Lee, and, stopping him, they refused to go into the fight unless General Hood commanded them. General Lee at once ordered that he be restored to his command, and he rode to the head of his brigade in the midst of a joyful ovation.

It is equally true that few brigades have had the personal love and care as that Texas brigade had from Hood. He knew every man in the brigade, could call him by his name, and ever had a pleasant remark for any he met. He was very careful of their comfort, looking after every detail very much as if caring for his own family. He never ordered them to go where he would not lead them, and his word could have sent them into the most appalling danger war can offer. At Sharpsburg his brigade lost over sixty per cent. in killed and wounded, while one regiment had lost over eighty-four per cent. Nine color bearers had been shot down one after another, but still the brigade preserved the flag, and stayed on the battlefield all the day after the fight.

My connection with the Army of Northern Virginia ended soon after the Battle of Fredericksburg, and I saw General Hood no more while he remained in that army. At that time, even though I had not yet been very closely associated with him, I had come to have not only the highest respect for his military skill, but had come to recognize the great generosity of his nature, which often led to the remark that he possessed a heart as big as that of an ox. I had learned that he never stood upon military etiquette in battle, and was ever ready to help a command out, if it got into a tight place, whether it belonged to his own organization or not, rather than lose the opportunity of rendering service by waiting to consult higher authorities, and was wholly regardless of who had the glory of the deed.

He remained with the Army of Northern Virginia until shortly before the Battle of Chickamauga, when he went with General Longstreet to the Army of Tennessee to help General Bragg. He was then hardly able to ride at the head of his command, having not fully recovered from the removal of a piece of the bone of his left arm, which was necessitated by a wound received at Gettysburg. Notwithstanding his little more than convalescent condition, he took part in the Battle of Chickamauga with his accustomed energy and success until he was struck in the thigh by an explosive bullet, which necessitated the amputation of his leg a few inches below the hip joint. When told after the amputation that he could not live, he cheerfully and determinedly replied that he would live, and the world knows how well he kept that promise.

This wound was received the 20th of September, 1863, and in February or March, 1864, he was made lieutenant-general, and assigned to a corps in the Army of Tennessee, formerly commanded by General D.H. Hill, of which I had been adjutant-general. In his order taking command of the corps, I was named as assistant-adjutant-general, and was made custodian of all his public papers, with orders to examine all dispatches, and trouble him with nothing I could attend to myself. During the six months I messed with him, I daily discovered some new admirable trait in his character, that made me highly appreciate being so near him. I found him always courteous to his staff officers, and very considerate of their comfort, but he never spared them in action any more than he did himself.

Though he came to the corps on crutches, he displayed all the energy and activity in attending to the duties of his larger command that had been so noticeable in his care of his Texas brigade, and this never slackened on the campaign with Johnston from Dalton to Atlanta. I was with him in all the fights made during this campaign and wondered at his great activity in his crippled state.

About midnight on the 17th of July a telegram for General Hood was handed me, and on opening it I found it to be from the President, ordering General Hood to take command of the Army of Tennessee, to succeed General Johnston. Almost appalled at the news, I carried the telegram at once to General Hood, who seemed to feel very much as I did in the matter. The next morning at breakfast, he read it aloud to several persons who were present. Among these was a Confederate Congressman from Kentucky, who immediately remarked, "Surely, Hood, you're not going to accept." General Hood replied, "I am a soldier and know nothing but to obey orders, and do the best I can. If I fail, the responsibility is with the power that gave the order; if I succeed his is the glory."

It was known to all the corps commanders that Johnston intended to attack Sherman's army within the next few days, the matter having already been fully discussed and the plan of battle perfected in a council of war. The order came as a perfect surprise to everybody, and was regarded in the light of a disaster to General Hood himself. The three corps commanders, Hood, Hardee, and A. P. Stewart, rode to General Johnston's headquarters early in the morning and in a body, requested General Johnston to retain the command of the army until the contemplated fight should be made. General Johnston replied that he understood his orders to turn over the command of the army to General Hood to be peremptory, and he could not so far disregard them. They then asked if he would consent to make the fight if they could get permission from the President. He replied that he would. And a telegram was sent, asking Mr. Davis to hold up the order for the transfer of the army, until the contemplated fight could be made. This telegram was signed by Generals Hood, Hardee and A. P. Stewart. The reply came promptly, and repeated that the orders were peremptory, and that Johnston had already had five months in which to attack Sherman.

In obedience to the order Hood at once assumed command of the army, and prepared to attack Sherman on Johnston's plan, while his army was divided and its back to Peachtree Creek. And had Hood's orders been promptly obeyed, in all human probability, the 20th of July, 1864, would have marked the date of a complete victory of the Confederacy. To retrieve the failure of the 20th, General Hood made another plan for the 22nd, which promised success, but here again the same officer failed Hood's expectations. The second failure necessitated the battles of the 28th and 30th, which culminated in the evacuation of Atlanta.

General Hood then moved his army to Lovejoy Station, where it rested and recuperated for several weeks, while preparations were being made for the campaign in Sherman's rear. Just before the army started on this campaign, Mr. Davis made a visit to General Hood's headquarters. After the army had started on its march, I rode up to General Hood's headquarters in time to see him bid farewell to Mr. Davis, and mount his horse to follow the army. From the events which followed, the army drew the conclusion that on this visit, Mr. Davis had given implied if not explicit orders for Hood to attack the Federals wherever he should find them.

I still retained my position with the corps, but I frequently saw General Hood after he became commander of the Army of Tennessee, and I always found him the same cheerful, courteous gentleman, patiently attending to the irksome details of his command, in spite of the many inconveniences caused by his mutilated body.

When we arrived in Columbia, Tennessee, we found the town occupied by the enemy, and General Hood prepared to give them battle, but before the intended attack could be made, they evacuated the city and crossed Duck River. Then General Hood conceived a plan, that for brilliancy and promise, was never excelled by Stonewall Jackson. With General Hardee's corps, commanded by Cheatham, A.P. Stewart's corps, commanded by himself, and General Ed. Johnson's division of S.D. Lee's corps (formerly Hood's corps), he moved up the river several miles, and crossed over for the purpose of cutting off the retreat of the enemy at Spring Hill, some fifteen miles on the pike to Nashville, leaving S.D. Lee at Columbia with one division of his corps, and most of the artillery of the army to entertain the Federals across the river. General Lee carried out his instructions by keeping up a fire on the enemy all day, and driving back their pickets far enough from the river to allow him to build a pontoon bridge, and cross his men over the river shortly after dark. Then we started in pursuit of the retreating Federals, intending to attack as soon as we should come up with them, fully expecting the remainder of the army to be in front of them, barring their retreat at Spring Hill.

In the meantime, General Hood had carried out his plan successfully so far as to beat the enemy to Spring Hill, except the one division already stationed there, and had his orders been promptly obeyed, this division would have been destroyed or captured, and the eight hundred wagons parked there would have fallen into our hands in less than one hour after the order was given. This would have left General Schofield with the remainder of the army, with General Hood between him and his base, and General Lee in his rear, with no hope of escape.

Before Hood realized that his orders had not been obeyed, night came on, and his army lay in line of battle parallel to the pike between four and eight hundred yards from it; when the order had been that it should be across it. In this position they remained until the whole Federal army had passed, moved their wagon train, and escaped. There had been great blundering somewhere, though it seemed that every man in the army should have known the condition of affairs. We of Lee's division expected every moment to come up with the enemy and capture them with the greatest ease. We had not the slightest intimation that the plan had failed, until we came up with General Ed Johnson's division of our corps, and the privates, who appreciated the fact that some one had criminally blundered, began calling out, "General Lee, it wasn't our fault." I heard General Ed Johnson say that during the night, he could have routed the entire Federal army with only his division, but was not permitted to attack them. He said that they came along the pike in the greatest confusion, and some straggling from the road, had come into his lines and were captured.

Major Hamilton and Major Blanton, both of Hood's staff, told me afterward, that they had each carried an order to General Cheatham to throw his army across the turnpike, and attack the Federals at Spring Hill before night, and that each of them had carried the order the second time, and later, after night, when the attack could no longer be made, the order had been for General Cheatham to place his men across the pike, thus cutting off the retreat of Schofield.

At the General Reunion of the United Confederate Veterans at New Orleans in 1903, I had a long talk with General S. D. Lee, who was too much indisposed to go out, and asked me to remain with him until bed time. In the course of our conversation, he asked me who I thought was to blame for the failure at Spring Hill. I told him that I had always considered that it was due to General Cheatham's failure to carry out General Hood's orders. He replied, "Yes, that's the general impression, and General Cheatham died letting the country put the blame on him." He then told me that General John C. Brown, of Tennessee, was the man who was at fault. I protested that he must be mistaken, for General Brown was one of our ablest officers and one who always did his full duty. He then explained that General Brown was very popular in that part of Tennessee, and the people of the country, to show their appreciation of the prospective freedom from Yankee domination, had made him a great many presents of liquors, and while he was not habitually intemperate, he had, on that occasion, become too much intoxicated to attend to his duties. He then gave me his authority for the information, which is above question.

The Federals having escaped to Franklin, Tennessee, General Hood followed and attacked them there, and the battle which followed was one of the bloodiest of the whole war. During the night the enemy evacuated the place and the next day we followed them to within sight of Nashville. In the fights around Nashville, Hood was successful until the very last, when his line unaccountably gave way in the middle, and the retreat became a rout.

I saw General Hood frequently on the retreat from Nashville to Tupelo, Mississippi, where he left the army and went to report to Richmond, and then I saw him no more until January of 1867, in New Orleans, where he was in business.

During the time I served on General Hood's staff, and received and delivered his mail, I saw many letters from the direction of which I inferred that he had a very particular lady correspondent, and it was currently reported in the army, that he was engaged to be married to a very wealthy lady of South Carolina. While in New Orleans on my way to Texas, I looked General Hood up, and found him in the office in the second story of a hardware house. Before I had time to knock, he saw me through the glass door, and called out cordially, "Come in Major." I had read in a newspaper a false report of his marriage, and when I offered my congratulations, he smiled sadly and said, "Things have changed, Major. Then I was a general in the Confederate Army; now I am a poor man without a country," thus telling the whole pathetic story. This was my last meeting but one, with him before his death.

Lieutenant-General James Longstreet

The career of General Longstreet would be of interest if it had nothing more than his long connection with the Army of Northern Virginia to recommend it. He was with that army from the time it came into existence until it surrendered, while no one of anything like so great prominence was connected with it for one-half so long. And his book, *From Manassas to Appomattox*, is the best authority on the history of that army that has ever been before the public.

It was at Centerville, while he commanded a division of General Johnston's army, that I first met him. I saw him in all the early movements of the army, and greatly admired him. He was a handsome man of fine physique, something under forty-five. I remember particularly his keen sense of the ridiculous, his enjoyment of the wit of others, and his distaste for speaking in public even on the most informal occasions. He was as bashful as a boy, and would gladly lay hold on any one he could get to take his place or excuse him when serenaded by the band and called on for a speech. He was hardly more fluent in writing than in speech, his particular readiness being in fighting. Most of these impressions were gathered from observations during his frequent visits to General D. H. Hill, whose military ability and moral character he admired as much as he enjoyed his delightful wit. I often heard these two men in discussion of men and measures that were not intended for the public.

At the Battle of Seven Pines he was nominally in command of the right wing of General Johnston's army. General D.H. Hill was to open the fight on the right with his division, with Longstreet's five brigades close behind to support him. General Longstreet told General Hill that he was not going to interfere with him in the immediate fight, and if he needed any more troops, to send to him for them. General Hill accepted this offer, and sent me after them, one brigade at a time until I had put all Longstreet's command in the fight. The confidence placed in General Hill's ability was fully justified, for the battle on the right was a perfect success for us, and that night we slept in the enemy's camp.

General Longstreet's command did not fight next to ours around Richmond, but history is a better chronicler than I of the excellent service he rendered there as well as at South Mountain and Sharpsburg. I saw him at Sharpsburg as cool and composed as if on dress parade. I could discover no trace of unusual excitement except that he seemed to cut through his tobacco at each chew. He was near by when a cannon ball cut off both forelegs of General Hill's horse a little above the knees. The horse fell forward, and for an appreciable space of time it was very uncertain on which side he would finally fall. When he wavered to one side General Hill would try to dismount on the other, and before he could do so the horse would seem as if he were going to fall that way, and this went on for some little time, until it began to look like a game of see-saw. All the time, General Longstreet was watching the performance and giving such advice as, "This side, Hill; no, the other; get off over his head, Hill, slide off behind."

I saw him briefly during his short stay in the Army of Tennessee, when he was sent to help General Bragg, just before the Chickamauga fight. At the council called by Mr. Davis after the battle, to learn why the victory had not been followed up, he incurred the displeasure of General Bragg by his unqualified statement of some humiliating facts as to that general's behavior during the fight. After that I saw him no more until I saw him in New Orleans in 1867.

About that time, the old Confederate soldiers who had taken no part in politics on account of the obnoxious oath of allegiance, were inquiring of their leaders what to do in the matter. I saw in a newspaper quite a number of replies given by the Confederate generals, none of them more than twenty lines long. Among them was one given by General Longstreet in which I could detect nothing essentially different from those given by the others. I could see in it not a glimmer of disloyalty to the South, but some editor, seeking for something sensational, dissected and manipulated it, until its original elements seemed to be changed, and then he raised the cry of disloyalty, which was later taken up by others, and finally prepared the way for him to go into the Republican party.

I could never believe that General Longstreet was not as true to the principles for which he had so gallantly fought, as any man in the South, and I asked Major Goree, who had served on Longstreet's staff throughout the war, to tell me what he knew of the matter. He said, in substance, that the Confederate leaders who lived in New Orleans, seeing that for Louisiana to become self governing, it must go Republican, and if they took no part in politics, the State must continue to be under Negro rule, but if they did take part, they could secure a White man's government even though it were Republican. And as General Longstreet was the most prominent of the old soldiers living there, and as it was known that General Grant, who was a kinsman of Longstreet, had made overtures to him, they put him forward as the leader, promising to stand by him. He then wrote an article for the papers, outlining the plan, and submitted it to the editor of a prominent New Orleans paper for publication, this editor having been in the agreement. The paper did not publish the article, but came out in a most scathing editorial against Longstreet, which aroused the whole of New Orleans against him. His Confederates at once weakened and so determinedly avoided him, that for several days, he could not get a word with any of them. And finally, when he forced a meeting with one of them, and asked an explanation of this treatment, he replied, "Longstreet, we can't stand the racket," and then began the war on Longstreet in New Orleans. He was so entirely boycotted that, depending as he did upon his business for a support for himself and his family, he was reduced to the verge of starvation in that great city, for the liberty of whose people he had so often imperilled his life in battle. He was saved by the offer from General Grant, that if he would take the oath of allegiance, he would give him the position of collector of customs of New Orleans, which he accepted.

Though by this step, he completely lost all standing in New Orleans, he never lost the respect and devotion of the old soldiers all over the South, who had seen him give, too many times, the very highest evidence of devotion to their cause.

He was never invited to take any part in any way in the General Reunion of the United Confederate Veterans until the meeting in New Orleans in 1893, when it met in the Opera House, when it became known that he was in the audience and he was invited to a seat on the rostrum. When he passed up the aisle, his old Virginia soldiers raised an affectionate cheer, while many who owed their prominence and influence to accident kept their seats in silence. And again the same night, in a business meeting in Armory Hall, when thousands were present, Judge Watts, of Dallas, Texas, got the floor, and administered a very scathing and well-deserved rebuke to the management of the reunion for their treatment of Longstreet, and moved that a committee be sent to bring him to the rostrum. Some one in the audience replied that it was then 9 o'clock and General Longstreet's home was four miles away, and as he was in feeble health, he would very likely have retired for the night, and would not wish to be disturbed. But Judge Watts had struck the keynote of the feelings of the old soldiers, and they would not down until a committee had been appointed and sent to bring him. When in due time they returned with Longstreet, his entrance was hailed with prolonged cheering, and as he passed up the aisle to the platform, there was such a rush to shake hands with him, that the business feature of the meeting came to an unceremonious end.

On the next day when the old soldiers paraded the streets, General Longstreet's carriage came up a side street and halted for him to see the parade. When it was discovered by the soldiers, the cheering began again, and many left the ranks to gather about the carriage, until there were long gaps in the line left by the great number who were now doing honor to the old hero.

APPENDIX
The Confederate Soldier in the Ranks[1]
by Major-General D.H. Hill, C.S.A.

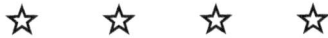

☆   ☆   ☆   ☆

Soldiers of the Army of Northern Virginia,
Ladies and Gentlemen:

It is meet and proper that the Association of the veterans of the noblest, truest and bravest army that the sun ever shone upon, should assemble in the Capital of the late Confederacy. It is eminently fitting, too, that it should meet in the Capital of Virginia, since its name and fame are inseparably associated with three illustrious Virginians. It was a Virginian who first organized it and sent it upon its wonderful career of victory; it was a Virginian, who, at its head, held at bay for three years the army recruited from the four quarters of the globe, and who, with ever-decreasing forces, *fought the world in arms;* it was a Virginian, who, with portions of this famous army made those stealthy marches to the rear and struck those terrible blows, which so astonished the world. We remember

---

1. This address was delivered on the evening of October 22, 1885 in Richmond, Virginia before the Virginia Division of the Association of the Army of Northern Virginia.

that it was a Virginian, whose eloquence most fired the hearts of the Colonists against British aggression; that it was a Virginian, who moved in that Continental Congress for a declaration of independence; that it was a Virginian who wrote that declaration; that it was a Virginian, who led the armies of the rebellion against Great Britain; that it was a Virginian, who so expounded the principles of the Constitution as to make that instrument acceptable to the American people; that it was a Virginian who presided over the court established under that Constitution with such ability and impartiality that he is to-day regarded as the wisest, greatest and purest of the Chief Justices of the United States. We remember with great pride that one-half of the life of the nation from Washington to Lincoln – thirty-six of the seventy-two years – was passed under the administration of Virginia Presidents. We remember with reverential awe, the father of his country, the Virginia-born Washington, of whom Wellington said that he was the grandest and sublimest, and yet the plainest and simplest character in history. Concerning whom Byron made the pathetic lament that the earth had no more seed to produce another like unto him.

But, though, from the settlement at Jamestown to the present hour, proud memories and glorious traditions cluster around the beautiful women and illustrious men of Virginia, I honestly believe that the most heroic portion of her history is from 1861 to 1865, when she so grandly bared her bosom to the hostile blow, and bore with such sublime patience the desolation of her soil and the slaughter of the noblest and best of her sons. The Army of Northern Virginia! So let it be! Let the grand old State and the grand old army bear the same name, and may their fame be linked together forever and forever!

Others have spoken before your Association of the great battles and the great leaders of the civil war. Mine be the grateful task to talk of the unknown and unheralded private in the ranks. The picture of him rises before you all – the keen, patient, quizzical, devil-may-care face, the brimless slouch hat, the fragment of a coat, the ragged breeches, the raw-hide shoes, unless some lucky find on the battlefield had given better foot-gear (and Johnny always was particular about his under-pinning). When he had his trusty rifle and well-filled cartridge box, he considered himself splendidly clad with half a uniform and a whole pair of shoes. He was self-reliant always, obedient when he chose to be, impatient of drill and discipline, critical of great movements and small movements, the conduct of the highest and lowest officers, from Mars Robert down to the new-fledged lieutenant. He was proud of his regiment, scornful of odds, uncomplaining of fatigue, ungrumbling at short rations, full of strange drollery and mockery at suffering.

Such was the Confederate soldier between '61 and '62. before battle and disease had swept away the flower of the Southern youth. He had the *élan* of the Frenchman, the rollicking humor of the Irishman, the steadfastness of the Englishman or German, and the dogged perseverance of the Scotchman. He was ready to charge a battery with the wild Rebel yell or to receive a charge with the imperturbable calmness of Wellington's veterans at Waterloo. He had the best characteristics of the best fighters of the best races of the whole earth. The independence of a country life, hunting, fishing and the mastery of slaves, gave him large individuality and immense trust in himself. Hence he was unsurpassed and unsurpassable as a scout and on the skirmish line. Of the shoulder-to-shoulder courage, born of drill and discipline, he knew nothing, and cared less. Hence, on the battle-field, he was more of a free lance than a machine. Who ever saw a Confederate line advancing that was not crooked as a ram's horn? Each ragged Rebel yelling on his own hook and aligning on himself.

But there is as much need of the machine-soldier as of the self-reliant soldier, and the concentrated blow is always the most effective blow. The erratic effort of the Confederate, grand, brilliant and heroic though it was, yet failed to achieve the maximum result, just because it was erratic. Moreover, two serious evils attended that excessive egotism and individuality, which came to the Confederate through his training, association and habits. He knew when a movement was false and a position was untenable, and he was too little of a machine to give in such cases that whole-hearted service which might have redeemed the blunder. The other evil was an ever-growing one. His disregard of discipline and independence of character made him often a straggler, and the fruit of many a victory was lost by straggling. I believe that with his exalted patriotism, his high sense of honor and his devotion to duty, the Confederate soldier would have submitted to any just and reasonable discipline imposed by honest and intelligent officers.

But too many of these officers were looking for political preferment after the war to permit a uniform system of government to become practical and possible. We needed, too, what our enemies had, an old army, a body of veterans, as a model of obedience, and as a nucleus for the formation of other troops like unto themselves. We needed the camps of instruction which our enemies had, the drill masters, and the months given to training and discipline of their recruits, while ours had of necessity to be hurried to the front. The South had rushed into the war absolutely destitute of everything, save the courage of its people, which makes a military nation. We had no foundries, no machine shops, no factories, no powder mills, no roller mills, no paper mills, no means of making tents and camp equipage. The paper upon which the ordinances of secession of the respective States were written came from the North; the ink and pens with which they were written came from the North. We had no iron works for casting cannon, no gun factories for small arms, no establishments to manufacture powder, none in which to make caps for muskets and rifles. Even after the Battle of Manassas the question of returning to the old flint-lock was seriously discussed. The spinning wheel and the handloom were the chief dependence for furnishing clothing to the troops. The country tan-yard and the country cobbler could alone furnish them with shoes. There was not in all the South a factory for making blankets for the soldiers, who had to endure the bitter rigors of the winter in the border States. We had no ships upon the ocean to draw supplies from abroad, while our enemies could recruit their armies and their war material from the continents of the whole globe and from the far off isles of the sea. From first to last, ours was the worst equipped, the worst fed, the worst clothed, and the worst organized army in the world; that of our enemy was the best equipped, the best organized, the best cared for, and the most pampered arms of the nineteenth century.

It is the grandest tribute that mortal man can pay to our soldiery to say that they knew of the tremendous difference between their condition and that of their foes, and *that they were contemptuous of it.* They believed that

their courage, their fortitude, their patience and their devotion to duty, would more than make up for all deficien-
cies in organization, equipment, material and numbers. I
will give some examples of these grand characteristics.
On the 31st May, 1862, my division attacked the Federal
division of General Casey, having a pentagonal redoubt in
which were ten guns. On each side of the redoubt were
rifle-pits, which could only be reached by struggling
through an abattis of from twenty to one hundred yards
in width. Three Federal batteries in rear had a murderous
fire upon the road and upon all the approaches to the
works. The recent heavy rains had made the ground almost a quagmire. But on our gallant fellows went floun-
dering through the mud and slush, wading through water
three and four feet deep, scarcely able to advance, had
there been no foe in front. But they were mown down at
every step by cannon shot, shell, grape and canister; they
were mown down by the musketry fire of men calmly
awaiting them under the protection of earthworks and
obstructions. On and on went those nameless heroes of
unrecorded graves. The Fourth North Carolina regiment,
with bloody loss, captured a section of artillery in the
road and made way for Carter's battery, which came up
to the relief of our struggling infantry. Now began that
awful, that wonderful contest between five guns sinking
almost to the axle at every fire against sixteen guns in
position. It was a brief artillery duel, for Couch's division
was coming up in massive columns to the aid of the sore-
ly pressed Casey, and by my own express order, Carter
turned his fire upon the approaching masses of infantry;
every shell burst in the right place, every solid shot struck
in the right place; the ranks broke and sought shelter in
the woods on our right and in the abattis on our left. There

was no further advance by the Federals up the Williamsburg road after Carter turned his guns upon their infantry.
All this time the sixteen guns were remorselessly pelting
the five guns of the King William artillery, and his hith-
erto untried men were subjected to an ordeal which few
veteran artillerists will stand: that of receiving, without
returning, an artillery fire. But there was no flinching with
these splendid fellows, and they kept steadily to their
work on the infantry until their concealment in the brush
enabled the King William boys to give tit for tat to the
artillerists in blue. But relief now came to Carter's men
for a time at least; the advance of our infantry drove
Casey's men from the redoubt and the rifle pits, cut
Couch's division in two, turned part of it off to join Sumner and sent the other part streaming to the rear. The
fight began at 1 o'clock, and by 3 o'clock, my division,
without any assistance whatever, had captured Casey's
camp and earthworks, had taken ten pieces of artillery
and two hundred prisoners, and had defeated or checked
all the heavy reinforcements sent to Casey, at least two
divisions of succoring forces. And now, the first time, our
exhausted men got help. The Palmetto Sharpshooters, of
R. H. Anderson's brigade, Longstreet's division, under
Colonel Jenkins, came up. Some twenty minutes later, R.
H. Anderson reported to me with the Fourth, Fifth and
Sixth South Carolina regiments. Jenkins had gone to my
extreme left, and there the Twenty-seventh Georgia, of
my division, was attached to his regiment. Jenkins and
Anderson fought their way through the abattis in front of
the second line of intrenchments to which the defeated
had retired, captured that line and joining their forces,
held a brief consultation. Anderson took the Fourth and
Fifth South Carolina regiments with him, and went off to

to sweep down the rail road, giving Jenkins the Sixth South Carolina with orders to follow up the dirt road. With these three regiments – Palmettos, Sixth South Carolina and Twenty-seventh Georgia (1,800 men in all) – Jenkins began that march of victory, which has had but few parallels in history. He had to fight Heintzleman's corps, minus Berry's brigade, and such fragments of Key's corps as could be rallied. The enemy was dazed, bewildered and demoralized by Casey's defeat, so that the reinforcements did not fight as well as Casey's men had done. One of Casey's brigadiers said in his report, that he had seen Heintzleman's men break when they had hardly felt the Rebels.

Everything gave way before the three regiments and the masses of the enemy were steadily driven to the intrenched camp. At one time, Jenkins was confronted by a larger force than his own, while columns of attack were forming on each flank. He rushed at the *pas de charge* upon those in front, broke them, and then facing about, attacked in flank one of the columns flanking him and routed it. The other column disappeared. The pursuit ceased with darkness and Heintzleman boasted in his report that the Rebels got no further than the woods in which he and Keyes had gathered together 1,800 men. All the Federal reports speak of the overwhelming numbers of the Rebels that came upon them and lament that they had but 11,500 men to meet these fearful odds. Those words, "overwhelming numbers," applied by the Federals to every lost field, are most expressive. Johnny had a way of multiplying himself when he was in a good fighting humor and then he appeared very numerous; and when he had anything like a chance he was a very overwhelming sort of fellow.

All day Sunday and Sunday night General J. J. Peck, of the Federal army, had strong working parties strengthening the intrenched camp and making it more secure for the eleven thousand five hundred men who had sought refuge there. The success of the first day was not followed up on the second day. The wounding of our illustrious commander and other causes prevented an united attack upon Sumner, which must have crushed him. There was no fighting the second day to speak of except by Pickett, who started on his own accord and stopped when he pleased, or after he had driven the enemy to the brush, as he expressed it.

Seven Pines was not altogether a barren victory. It delayed McClellan until Jackson was brought upon his flank. It gave a splendid exhibition of dash and courage, and that had a most inspiriting effect upon the subsequent campaign.

Longstreet's division lost five hundred men; mine, 2,992, out of nine thousand men engaged. The Sixth Alabama and the Fourth North Carolina lost sixty per cent. of the men brought into action. Carter's battery lost fifty-nine per cent.

I was looking at the battery and was within ten yards of it, when a shell exploded just before the muzzle of one of its pieces, and all the men at it and the horses at the limber went down before it. They seemed to me all huddled together "in one red burial blent." An officer ran up and pulled out one live man from the confused pile. Two men were killed, five wounded, and two horses were killed by that one explosion. The wounded appeared, for the time being, to be paralyzed, as only one was pulled out at first. This was the most destructive shot I had ever seen up to that time, but I afterwards saw one worse at

Malvern Hill and one worse at Sharpsburg. It was the enemy's artillery in all three cases that was so deadly. This havoc in Carter's battery was in the pentagonal redoubt after its capture.

Two-thirds of the loss in Rodes' brigade was after Casey's works had been taken and his division and Couch's had been driven off. Berry's brigade, of Kearney's division, had been turned off into the slashes when Carter's fire had made a direct advance impracticable. There it was joined by one of Abercrombie's regiments, and possibly by rallied fragments of the defeated divisions, and securely sheltered behind large trees and heavy fallen timber, they kept up a murderous fire upon Rodes's men in the open field, though the advance of Anderson and Jenkins had cut them off from their comrades. These Federals escaped after nightfall by taking a circuitous path through the woods, round by Anderson's saw-mill.

It was said for a time that Casey was surprised and that his division was defeated by a sudden rush of mine. His own report and the reports of all his officers show that there was nothing of the kind. He had been waiting for us for hours with his men and guns in position. The sudden rush began at 1 o'clock, and Casey's works were captured at 3 o'clock. It is a misnomer to call a deadly struggle for two hours a sudden rush. It is unjust to my division, as well as to that opposing me, to say that Casey's men fought badly. They fought better than the reinforcements sent to help them.

Fowler Hamilton, a jolly dragoon officer, was asked in the Mexican war by some of the newly arrived troops, "Are the Mexicans brave?"

"They are brave enough for me," replied he.

Casey's men were brave enough for me, and he himself was a veteran of approved courage and conduct. He seems to have been one of the very last to abandon his earthworks.

The Battle of Seven Pines is a fine illustration of the prowess of untrained, untutored and undisciplined Southern soldiers. The great battles of Europe, in which veterans were engaged, show a loss of from one-tenth to one-fourth of those engaged. At Seven Pines our raw troops lost one-third of their number without flinching, moving steadily on to victory. The true test of the loss in battle is the number of casualties before the shouts of triumph rend the sky; for it has often happened that the chief loss of the defeated has been from the murderous fire upon their disorganized, unresisting, and huddled together masses. This has always been so when the defeat has been the result of a flank movement, or when a brilliant cavalry charge has followed up the rout.

But my theme deals with the individual private in the ranks and I will therefore give some personal anecdotes, which I know to be true, and are not sensational clap-trap for the occasion. After the capture of Casey's camp, one of my staff went with a litter to remove a private in the ranks, whom he had known at school.

"No," said the wounded man, "let me alone, Ratchford, I am mortally wounded. Carry off some one who will live to fight for his country another day." Then waving off his comrade with a feeble effort of his poor, dying hand, he said, "Good-bye, Ratchford," while the white lips parted in a farewell smile.

The world has wondered at and has praised for two hundred and ninety-nine years the grand self-denial of the dying Sir Philip Sidney, who gave the cup of water intended for himself to the wounded soldier that was looking longingly at it and said, "Friend, thy wants are greater than mine." The world has done well to preserve this sublime instance of unselfishness, but it was an unselfishness born of sympathy with present suffering appealing to him. The unselfishness of the Confederate was born of an abstract love of country looking away from the present to the future weal of our dear Southland. Who does not see that the self-denial of Private Addison Jones, of the Fifth North Carolina regiment, was of a higher and nobler type than the self-denial of the chivalric knight, the ideal hero of song and of story?

I will give some illustrations of an authentic character of the coolness and self-possession of the private in the ranks. From Colonel Sweitzer, of McClellan's Stall. I got under a flag of truce an anecdote of one of my couriers at Seven Pines. In carrying an order from me through the woods, he came unexpectedly upon a regiment, whose uniform made him feel blue. However, he kept up a bold front and asked: "What regiment is that?"

"Seventh Massachusetts," was the reply.

"All right," said the courier, "the orders are to hold your position at all hazards." Then he turned off into the woods before the blue-coats recovered their surprise sufficiently to give a harmless volley after him. I may not have the right name of the Federal regiment, but by inquiry I found out that of the courier; for, modest as brave, he had not boasted of his adventure. He was Hector Bowden, of Loudoun county, Virginia. Poor fellow! his was a sad fate, for on a secret visit to his parents, he was murdered by the Tories of Means' gang.

One other incident of the same kind. After the defeat of Porter at Cold Harbor, and while his men were huddled together in a confused mass in the woods after dark, they were told to encourage them, that Richmond had been captured and forthwith began to cheer vociferously. One of my couriers thinking that cheering could only come from victors, rode in among them and was greeted with the question: "Have we got Richmond?"

"Yes;" answered he, "*we* have got Richmond," and escaped undercover of their shouts and rejoicing. That courier was John Chamblin and Richmond has got him, if he has not got Richmond.

An anecdote showing the kind of wit which characterized the rollicking, careless, undisciplined boys of 1861, may not be out of place here. The story has been often told and many regiments have been credited with it. But I know the very time and the very regiment to which the anecdote belongs. At Yorktown, a colonel called out his regiment, formed it in line and began to scold the men savagely for some breach of discipline. In the midst of his vituperation a donkey began an unmerciful bray, when a unanimous shout came up from the impenitent and sorrowless gray-coats, "Hold on, Colonel, one at a time, one at a time." There is a delicacy of insinuation about this reply, which makes it unsurpassed and unsurpassable. No! I was not that colonel, though I could tell of as grievous a mishap to myself did not modesty forbid. I will tell rather of some other glorious exploits of the ragged Rebels.

At Boonsboro, or South Mountain, my division, reduced to five thousand men by battle, disease, hard marching and want of shoes, was called upon to confront McClellan's army and to hold Turner's Gap against two corps of that army, while two other corps were in supporting distance. The immense wagon-yard and parks of reserve artillery of Lee's whole army were at the foot of the mountain on the west side. General Lee himself, with Longstreet's command, was at Hagerstown, thirteen miles off. A thin curtain of men extending for miles along the crests of the mountains on that bright Sabbath day in September, was all we had to check a vast, perfectly organized and magnificently equipped army. There was nothing else to save our trains and artillery; there was nothing else to prevent McClellan from cutting in between Lee and Jackson; there was nothing else to save Longstreet's corps from irretrievable ruin. That thin curtain once broken, the enemy would have full possession of all our supply trains and supplies – ordnance, commissary and quartermaster stores; worse still, the two wings of Lee's army would have been riven asunder, never to be reunited. But there were giants in those days of 1862, and the haggard, weary, worn-out private in the ranks was a hero in his own right, and capable of multiplying himself into overwhelming numbers. From 9 A.M. till 3:30 P.M. two brigades and three regiments held at bay Reno's corps (said officially to be fifteen thousand strong), which attacked on our right, moving on the old Braddock road. Then three very small brigades of Longstreet's command, in an exhausted condition from their hot and hurried march, came to our assistance. With their aid the crests of the mountain and the road were held. Reno was killed at nightfall in Wise's field, where the fight began in the morning, and within fifty yards of where our beloved Garland fell.

But on our left a commanding hill was lost before sundown. All the fighting before 5 o'clock was on our right, and the first reinforcements from Longstreet were turned off in that direction where the enemy advanced very cautiously, because advancing in the woods and constantly apprehensive of surprise from overwhelming numbers. In fact, the whole battle on the right and left was one of self-imposed illusions on the part of the Federals. McClellan had came into possession at Frederick of a copy of Lee's order directing Jackson to attack Harpers Ferry, and Longstreet and myself to proceed to Boonsboro. The copy found was the one directed to me, though I must disclaim here, as ever before, that I was the loser of it. According to this order, Longstreet was at Boonsboro, and not Hagerstown, on the morning of the 14th, and McClellan's people believed that the whole mountain was swarming with Rebels.

It is a curious fact that the map of this battle, prepared by the United States Bureau of Topographical Engineers in 1872, ten years after the battle, represents ten regiments and one battalion under Longstreet at the foot of the mountain, on the north side of turnpike and east side of the mountain. This, on the morning of the 14th September, before the fighting began. Longstreet did not have a man there at any time, and not one any where on the mountain till 3:30 P.M. I had forty men at the foot of the mountain on north side of the pike after 3 o'clock, but not a man before that time. These forty men were under command of Captain R.E. Park, of the Twelfth Alabama, now living in Macon, Georgia. To have produced the impression that there were ten regiments and one battalion here, these forty men must have been uncommonly *frisky,* and they must have multiplied themselves astonishingly, but unfortunately for us, not in overwhelming numbers. Burnside tells us that he sent two peremptory orders to Fighting Joe Hooker before he would move forward his corps. From the foot of the mountain, Fighting Joe watched the magnificent advance of the divisions of Meade and Hatch, followed by the division of Ricketts. The previous fighting had drawn all our men, except Rodes' brigade, to the south side of the pike, and it was posted on the commanding point of which I have spoken. Meade took his division, with the true instincts of the soldier, to the peak held by Rodes with 1,200 men. So resolutely was Meade met that he sent for Duryea's brigade, of Ricketts's division. Longstreet's broken down men were still arriving, and four hundred under Colonel Stevens went to the help of Rodes, and were in time to save him from being surrounded, but their combined effort could not save the peak, and the key of our position was lost. The steady advance of the other Federal divisions drove back by nightfall the remainder of Long-street's forces on the left of the pike to the very crest of the mountain. But the pike itself was still held, and the effort of the Federals to move up it met with a bloody repulse. So the retreat was effected without difficulty and without pursuit. The trains and artillery were saved, and the two wings of Lee's army were united at Sharpsburg.

There had been much straggling of Longstreet's men on that hot and dusty march from Hagerstown. Garnett estimates that in marching and countermarching, his brigade passed over twenty-two or twenty-three miles. The reports are very meagre as to the numbers that were brought into action at South Mountain. We must judge of the whole from the few authentic estimates that are given. The Seventeenth South Carolina reports 141 men in the fight; the First South Carolina 106 men; the Seventeenth Virginia 55 officers and men; the Nineteenth Virginia 20 men; the Eighteenth Virginia 120 men; the Fiftieth Virginia 80 men; the Eighth Virginia 34 men. Longstreet admits now that his reinforcements did not exceed four thousand men. I think that estimate very high. But admitting this number, and that it was equally divided on the two sides of the pike, then Fighting Joe Hooker was contending with fifteen thousand men against 3,200 men, more than half of them in a broken down condition. However, his powerful field glass gave Fighting Joe a good view of the battle, and he felt proud, as well he might, of the steady and gallant advance of his three divisions. He says in his report: "When the advantages of the enemy's position are considered and his *preponderating* numbers, the forcing of the passage of South Mountain will be classed among the most brilliant and satisfactory achievements of this army, and its principal glory will be awarded to the First Corps." The reader will please remember that the First Corps was "Fighting Joe's" corps. However, I am thankful to Fighting Joe for saying preponderating numbers, and not overwhelming numbers.

The advantages of the position were with the attack, and not the defence, as any practical soldier will say, who will carefully examine the ground.

General McClellan said officially: "The force opposed to me was D.H. Hill's division (15,000 men), and a part, if not the whole of Longstreet's, and, perhaps, a portion of Jackson's. Probably thirty thousand in all." It is always safe to give a divisor of three to any estimate made by General McClellan of the forces of his enemy. The General puts his attacking force in the two corps at thirty thousand. On the 14th September, 1862, I would have given that number a multiplier of two. An attacking column is apt to take on the appearance of overwhelming numbers.

South Mountain was heralded abroad by our antagonists as a great victory. Favors of that sort had been few and far between, and this seemed to call for special gratulation and congratulation. Mr. Lincoln telegraphed the next day to General McClellan: "God bless you and all with you. Destroy the Rebel army, if possible." This is a model dispatch, and is a beautiful illustration of the meaning of St. James in the tenth verse of the third chapter of his epistle, which you can read when you go home.

But Sharpsburg affords, as I think, the best illustration of the pluck, dash and stubborn fighting of the privates in the ranks. Lee's army was never so small. It had fought McClellan from Richmond to Harrison's Landing on James River. It had fought Pope from the Rappahannock to the Potomac. It had given a new experience to this young warrior, who, like Lockinvar had come gaily out of the West and had only seen the backs of his enemies, and had there learned to scorn all thoughts of lines of retreat. I suspect that the young man did not *personally* gain any more knowledge in the East than he had done in the West about the faces of his foes, but the people he had about him did see those faces, and before he vanished amid the storm, he left behind him this military maxim, "for a line of retreat, the short cut is the safe cut."

The campaigns against McClellan and Pope had greatly reduced Lee's army. The order issued on crossing the Potomac excusing all barefooted men from marching had reduced it still more. So, at Sharpsburg, General Lee had only the hardiest, strongest and bravest of his Rebel boys. The straggling had been enormous. The chaff had been blown off and only the sound, solid wheat had been left.

General McClellan estimates Lee's army at Sharpsburg at 97,445. These numbers, he says, he got from General Banks, who had them from "prisoners, deserters and spies." The precision of this calculation strikes me as most admirable: 97,445, no more, no less. It was not a guess. Oh, no! General Lee's guess of the strength of his own army would have fallen short of this by more than 60,000. No, it was not a guess. It was obtained from "prisoners, deserters and spies." These generally count in round numbers, but on this occasion were minutely accurate. Why not 97,000 dry so? Why not 97,400? Why not 97,440? Who figured out the last five? I surmise that "the intelligent contraband" is responsible for this astonishing precision. The added five helped to swell up "the overwhelming numbers." It could not, would not, *should* not be omitted.

General McClellan puts his own forces at 87,464. He, too, must have been troubled with enormous straggling. For we find on page 98, Volume XIII, *Records of the Rebellion*, a statement from Quartermaster-General Rufus Ingalls, that he had furnished transportation for 190,185 officers and men of McClellan's army. This statement was made on the 1st day of October, 1862, fourteen days after the Battle of Sharpsburg and the wastage of that battle is not in the estimate. If we put McClellan's casualties at 12,000 in the battle, he must have had 202,185 on his rolls on the morning of Sharpsburg. For the same record shows a complaint from him that he had *not* received any reinforcements after the battle. If then there were but 87,164 at Sharpsburg, there were 105,021 elsewhere.

I have always contended that General Lee had less than 27,000 infantry and artillery in the Battle of Sharpsburg. He crossed the Potomac with nine divisions. As mine had not been in the Pope campaign and had there-

fore suffered less than the other eight from battle, disease
and fatigue, I supposed it to be one of the very largest,
and yet it had but little over 3,000 men in it at
Sharpsburg. As nine times 3,000 gives 27,000, I thought
that 27,000 was the maximum number in Lee's army. Dr.
Dabney, a very careful statistician, puts Lee's strength at
33,000 including the cavalry. My estimate, which I have
had to reduce, was of infantry and artillery alone.

On page 813 of this Volume XIII, I find Lee's
losses in killed and wounded in the Maryland campaign to
have been 10,291, of which, my division is credited with
2,902 or 28.19 per cent. of the whole. It is not reasonable
to suppose that this division should sustain more than
one-fourth of the entire loss of the army, if its strength
was not greater than one-ninth of the whole. It is true that
the loss at South Mountain fell largely upon my division,
but the loss there was probably as great in prisoners as in
killed and wounded, and the 10,291 loss is in killed and
wounded only. So I had two reasons for believing that my
division was the largest of the nine at Sharpsburg, and
that therefore Lee's infantry and artillery did not come up
to 27,000.

But the result can be reached in other ways, for
though the reports are most meagre on the Southern side,
we still have data enough to make an estimate different
from that of the prisoners, deserters and spies whom
General Banks saw.

General Lee crossed the Potomac with nine divisions, forty brigades, one hundred and sixty-six regiments
and nine battalions of infantry. Three divisions were made
out of two, so that at Sharpsburg, he had ten divisions
without having more brigades and regiments. We have
reports from five of these divisions: Early's division, four

brigades, 3,500 men; D.R. Jones's division, six brigades, 2,430 men; A.P. Hill's division, six brigades, 3,524 men; McLaws' division, five brigades, 2,832 men; D.H. Hill's division, five brigades, 3,008 men; total, 15,294 men.

From this number in twenty-six brigades of the forty in Lee's army, the single rule of three will give us 23,523 men as Lee's strength in infantry and artillery at the Battle of Sharpsburg. This is, of course, on the supposition that the ratio in the twenty-six brigades was the same for the other twenty-four. Let us examine this by the light from the reports of the brigades themselves, so far as they are given:

Robert Ransom, 1,600; Lawton, 1,150; Wof-ford, 854; Rodes's, 800; Barksdale, 800; Walker, 700; Trimble, 700; Hays, 550; Benning, 400; Cobb, 250; Stonewall, 250; Evans, 209; Kemper, 350; Garnett, 200. Total, 8,813.

The single rule of three gives the strength of the forty brigades on the ratio of these fourteen, to be 25,180. So the approximate results reached from the reports of division and brigade commanders differ only by 1,557 men.

Now let us see what estimate we can get from the reports of regimental commanders, so far as given in this same Volume XIII. We have:

Eleventh Georgia regiment, 140; Eighteenth Georgia regiment, 176; Fifty-third Georgia regiment, 276; Fiftieth Georgia regiment, 100; Tenth Georgia regiment, 134; Second and Twentieth Georgia regiments, 400; First Texas regiment, 226; Sixteenth Mississippi regiment, 228; First South Carolina regiment, 106; Seventh South Carolina regiment, 268; Seventeenth South Carolina regiment, 59; Hampton Legion, 77; Nineteenth Virginia regiment,

150; Eighteenth Virginia regiment, 120; Fifty-sixth Virginia regiment, 80; Seventeenth Virginia regiment, 55; Eighth Virginia regiment, 34. Total, 2,629.

General Lee had one hundred and sixty-six regiments, and nine battalions of infantry at Sharpsburg, say in round numbers, one hundred and seventy regiments of infantry. From the ratio of the eighteen regiments just given, we have for the whole one hundred and seventy regiments, 24,829. This differs from the estimate by brigades only by two hundred and *fifty-one* men. If we put our artillery at two thousand, we will have Lee's strength at Sharpsburg about 27,000. This estimate has been arrived at by four independent calculations: 1st. The strength and loss in my own division; 2d. The strength of the five divisions reported; 3d. The strength of fourteen brigades, including largest and smallest; 4th. The strength of eighteen regiments, including largest and smallest. Taking General McClellan's own estimate of his forces, 87,164, the boys in gray were outnumbered by sixty thousand. Not one of you who were on that terrible field will think even now, when calmly reviewing the awful scenes of that bloody day, that the odds against us was less than three to one. Who did not see again and again a thin Rebel line, scarcely a skirmish line, attack three heavy lines of battle with the utmost confidence, and come back again looking puzzled because the other fellows did not run? I will attempt no description of the wonderful deeds of valor performed by the hungry, ragged and broken down Rebels. Your own Patrick Henry could not do justice to it; my poor, stammering tongue would fall infinitely short of it. I have seen a plucky little bee-martin hover over, swoop down upon and peck at the ferocious hawk, and I have seen the grotesque movements of the great hulking bird to avoid the tiny beak of its tormentor. These old eyes of mine have watched that battle in the air, and these old eyes of mine looked upon the battle by the Antietam.

It is to the glory of Virginia that more than one-fourth of the infantry regiments, and about one-fourth of batteries actually engaged at Sharpsburg belonged to the Old Dominion. The best handling of artillery which I saw during the war was there, always excepting the King William battery at Seven Pines. That irrepressible and ubiquitous battery was at Sharpsburg also. I said in my official report, and I have said hundreds of time since, that this battery contributed largely to the defeat of Burnside's attack on our right and rear.

What shall I say of that wonderful campaign from the Wilderness to Petersburg, in which Lee's army killed and wounded more of their enemies than they had men in their own ranks? What shall I say of the ten months in the trenches, under a constant rain of shot and shell, endured by these privates in the ranks half fed, half clothed, destitute of all the usual appliances for a defensive siege; stifled at one time with heat and at another frozen with cold; fighting against ever-increasing odds – three times, five times, ten times, twenty times their own number – confronting in their want and misery the sleek soldiers of the most pampered army on the globe, luxurious in its comforts, magnificent in its appointments, and invincible in its serried masses? But those, our Confederates in the ranks fought on, suffered on, endured on, with no expectation of promotion or preferment; with no hope of ultimate success, each knowing surely that the end must be, at best, life and unrecognized prowess at worst, death and an unknown grave. We talk of the sufferings at Valley

Forge, and the American people should hold them in ever-lasting remembrance. But what were the sufferings of Washington's men in comparison with the sufferings of Lee's men? Yes, I feel that it is presumptuous in me to try to eulogize with words these martyrs without hope of reward or success – the Confederate soldiers in the ranks; but I yield to no man in my love, respect, and reverence for them.

And what shall be said of those unselfish patriots who were true to their colors to the last, when the ravages of armies had desolated their country, and the torches of bummers had left blackened chimneys as monuments over the buried treasures of a husband's and father's love? How can we sufficiently honor these men, who, knowing that their families, without food and without shelter, were starving to death or were living on the offal of the enemy's camps, who, knowing *even this,* yet still answered to roll call, yet still filled their places in the ranks, yet still faced death again and again, putting duty to country above duty to wife and children? Aye, how many of these poured out their heart's blood in that last despairing struggle, leaving those they loved more than life to the cold charities of a forgetful world? Hard must be the heart of that foeman which does not warm with a generous glow at this simple tale of sublime devotion to principle. And how should this story affect us, their comrades in danger and their partners in the same buoyant hopes and the same deep despair? May my arm be palsied by my side when it ceases to hold up the banner inscribed all over with their glorious deeds. May my tongue cleave to the roof of my mouth when it ceases to pronounce the praises of such matchless courage, unrivalled fortitude, and unselfish patriotism.

God bless the privates in the ranks now and forevermore!

Having an unwavering faith in the wisdom, justice, and mercy of God, I bow with adoring reverence to His decree which destroyed our hopes of Southern independence. I would not reverse His decree if I could do so. That would be wicked and presumptuous. All honorable Confederates render the truest allegiance to the obligations imposed upon them by the surrender. I believe that the most uncompromising rebels, yea, the bitterest rebels, if you choose to call them so, would be the *very* first to rally round the old flag in any just and honorable war. They have expressed the sincerest sympathy with the sufferings and misfortunes of illustrious foemen. They have rejoiced at the brilliant successes of many of their late antagonists, and they have contributed to those successes. But no generous conqueror wishes the conquered to forget their old ties and their old loves. No generous conqueror wishes us to disparage the grand heroism and the unparalleled constancy of the Confederates in the ranks. No generous conqueror expects us to underrate the ability of our great leaders because they were defeated, and unfairly fail to take into consideration that their defeat was due to overwhelming numbers. Every schoolboy knows of Thermopylae, and of Leonidas, defeated and slain; but who of you can tell the name of the victorious Persian commander of the Dori-Phori, who attacked him in front? Who of you remembers the name of the commander of the so-called Immortal Band which, having gone through a secret defile, attacked him successfully in rear?

The historian of the present looks only at victory and defeat. The historian of the past looks at all the surroundings. But even now we of the present, who have seen the great movements of our wonderful leaders, can look at those surroundings. Every one with Southern blood in his veins places in the front rank of the world's great commanders, the two modest men who sleep so quietly and so unostentatiously at Lexington, Virginia. Every one with Southern blood in his veins cherishes in his inmost soul the memory of their great deeds as a precious legacy to the land they loved so well.